CONTENTS

Acknowledgements

I would like to thank the following for their help in preparing this book: the French Department and the Research Support Fund, University of Wales, Swansea: Mme I. Minard, Bibliothèque Municipale, Vichy; Mme F. Lévèque, Bibliothèque "l'Heure Joyeuse", Paris; M. L. Gervereau and Mme L. Barbezet, Musée d'Histoire Contemporaine, Paris; M. et Mme J.-L. de Paepe; Professor K. Cameron; Mr A. Kelly.

CHILDREN AND PROPAGANDA

Il était une fois... : Fiction and Fairy Tale in Vichy France

Judith K. Proud

Foreword by H. R. Kedward

intellect™
Oxford, England

intellect

EUROPEAN STUDIES SERIES

General Editor: *Keith Cameron*

Humour and History	Edited by Keith Cameron
The Nation: Myth or Reality?	Edited by Keith Cameron
Regionalism in Europe	Edited by Peter Wagstaff
Women in European Theatre	Edited by Elizabeth Woodrough
Children and Propaganda	Judith Proud
The New Russia	Edited by Michael Pursglove
European Food	Edited by John Wilkins
Theatre and Europe 1957-1992	Christopher McCullough

Cover illustration: *'Populations abandonnées, faites confiance au soldat allemand!': Poster by T. Matejko, 1940.*
(All illustrations reproduced with the kind permission of Musée d'Histoire Contemporaine - BDIC, Paris)

First Published in 1995 by
Intellect Books
Suite 2, 108/110 London Road, Oxford OX3 9AW

Series editor: Keith Cameron
Production editor: Robin Beecroft
Copy editor: Dan Mayers

British Library Cataloguing in Publication Data Available

ISBN 1-871516-83-8

Printed and bound in Great Britain by Cromwell Press, Wiltshire

Foreword

Here is a book for the imagination. Here also is a book for the empiricist, for the cultural historian and for the textual critic. It is a study which any scholar working on the culture and politics of Vichy France will be excited to find, or equally would wish to have written. Its creative role in the analysis of propaganda within Occupied France is to direct us towards stories, images and myths which are associated with the world of childhood and in so doing illuminate the cultural praxis of the Vichy state, of collaborationism and anti-Semitism, which affected the whole population, young and old. If the starting point of Dr Proud's scholarly story is Charles Perrault's *Contes de ma mère l'Oye* of 1697, and the centre and end the propaganda of Vichy, the backdrop is the continuing receptivity of children and adults to the folklore of the miraculous and the ordinary, the terrifying and the reassuring, which can so easily be recruited for moral and political purposes. Vichy's appropriation of Perrault has its own specificity, but it also points to the wider function of folktales in any society and to the shifting discourse of childhood images from one social or political regime to another. The wish to imbue such images with a psychological permanence within our individual or collective development must always acknowledge the vulnerability of these images to political manipulation; indeed this vulnerability is no more and no less than a facet of their permanence. Dr Judith Proud demonstrates in impressive detail the ease with which the universal symbol becomes the polemical cipher; but under Vichy it went beyond a question of political adaptation. Behind it lay a certain ideological interpretation of the child's imagination.

There is much evidence to show that Right and Left in French politics, however defined, had actively disputed the mythologies of children's fiction from the French Revolution onwards. It was not only a rivalry of interest in the education, or manipulation, of the child, but increasingly an embittered conflict to free the child from external influences seen to be harmful and erroneous. If the republican, laïque, tradition was generally dominant within primary schools after the Ferry reforms, it held its own precisely against mythologies thought to be working on the child from the church, within the home or within a certain range of fictional material which incorporated a 'superstitious' view of the world. Conversely, nationalists and anti-republicans increasingly called for the young child to be set free, not from a set of fictional mythologies but from an attitude of mind which was held to devalue myth and imprison the child's imagination. Georges Bernanos, giving colourful expression to the ideology of the anti-republican Right in 1930, called the republican pedagogues 'les cuistres du siècle des cuistres' under whose pedantry the child would be ruthlessly confined to lessons on Republicanism and 'equality before the law', if 'the good Mr Perrault - let's call him Saint Perrault for he is surely in paradise - had not offered the exiled kings and queens the golden sanctuary of his fairly tales, the castles of Sleeping Beauty.' (*Noël à la Maison de France*, 1930, p.16). The intention of Bernanos in this 'little royalist book for Christmas' was to elevate the child's fairytale imagery to the level of transcendental political truth, anticipating the name of 'Vérité' given to the grandma in the version of Red Riding Hood so perceptively analysed by

Judith Proud. In this perspective the world of princes, giants and princesses is not a discreet realm of children's fantasy but one which constitutes the optimum social structure for France, past, present and future. 'What is a king?' Bernanos asks a young boy in Lorraine. 'A man on horseback who has no fear,' comes the reply. Bernanos comments, 'His father is republican, but no matter. Yes, my boy, you are right, a man on horseback ... with the youth of France behind him ...' For Bernanos the boy's reply is a political testament. He is wiser than his republican teachers. The child reigns, not in an inversionary saturnalian rite, but permanently by virtue of the imagination.

The conjuncture of Marshal Pétain and the world of the child that had been interpreted in this way, predates the Vichy regime by several weeks. From the start of the two-way relationship between Pétain and men, women and children devastated by the exode and the defeat, there is a cultivated infantilism by which the French people become his children and he their father and servant. Only secondly did he adopt 'le langage du Chef' (*Message*, 30 October 1940). Hagiographical writings, dedicated to Pétain, cemented this parental relationship both before 1940 and after his assumption of power, and Dr Proud quite rightly sees René Benjamin's *Le Maréchal et son peuple* (1941) as an extension, or further example, of the fairytale format, just as Gustave Hervé's *C'est Pétain qu'il nous faut* of 1936 was a forerunner. It remained for Charles Maurras to take what he saw as the logical step in *La Seule France* (1941) and to equate Pétain with truth, about which there could be no opinion. The child's imagination, as defined by the anti-republican Right, was already the repository of that truth, so that adults had only 'to become as little children' for the perfect symbiosis of Pétain and the people of France to be realised.

The regressive nature of infantilism severely marks the history of Vichy France, whatever its culural plurality. But there is more to the story than the elevation of Pétain , and selected other heroes and heroines, to fairytale status. The excellence of this book lies also in its textual reconstruction of the vicious scapegoating which took the children's fiction of Occupied France not only beyond Perrault but also well beyond Bernanos, too, who had already denounced the Right for its support for Franco in the Spanish Civil War. As Judith Proud's material all too clearly reveals, the organic ideology of the National Revolution, which put youth at the masthead of its ideology, was far from universal in its respect for the child's imagination: it depended on whether the child was French, and that was further refined into 'truly French'. Finally, to anchor the stories still further in Vichy's raison d'état, new alliances were prescribed for the characters in the authorised tales and comics, alliances which are presented by Dr Proud in their stark contrast to those of World War I.

In researching and writing this rich and suggestive book, Judith Proud has uncovered more than the mechanisms and aims of Vichy propaganda within children's fiction. She has shown that Vichy forced an entry into the 'lieu de mémoire' where the child's received images of mythical beings and events are stored, a place where myth and history, fantasy and reality are overlapping or even identical territories. The harm that can be done there by sectional dogma and dehumanisation is inestimable. Vichy was short-lived, but what it set out to do guaranteed that for many there would be no happy ending.

H R Kedward — *University of Sussex*, January 1995

Introduction

Il faut que vous sachiez que je compte absolument sur vous pour m'aider à reconstruire la France, à faire des Français un grand peuple loyal et honnête. Et je ne veux pas attendre que vous soyez devenus de grandes personnes pour vous demander de le faire

[I want you to know that I am counting on you absolutely to help me in the reconstruction of France and in making of the French people a great, loyal and honest nation. And I do not want to wait until you are grown up to ask you to do this]

(Philippe Pétain, Allocution of 13 October 1941).

When *Maréchal* Pétain, head of the French government, signed the Armistice with Germany on 22 June 1940, armed conflict with Germany may have ceased, but an offensive of another kind was just beginning. Based in its new headquarters in the many hotels and private villas of the fashionable spa town of Vichy in central France (Allier), the French government immediately set about consolidating its unusual position as political authority in a country of which a significant portion, including the capital itself, was under military occupation by the former enemy. The new offensive was not aimed at the Germans, but at the civilian population of France, and the weapons it used were not tanks and guns, but posters, pamphlets, books, films and radio broadcasts.

In Paris, too, plans were being put into motion to launch a series of propaganda campaigns targeting the French population as a whole, and more specifically the inhabitants of the occupied northern zone. Many of those involved were French nationals, eager missionaries of the collaborationist policy advocated by Vichy, or Fascist sympathisers only too pleased to find themselves free of the Left-wing yoke imposed by the Popular Front. The Germans, too, intended having their say in the behaviour and beliefs of the people of France, even if their plans for the country did not exactly match the vision of *la nouvelle France* that was to emerge from the *Révolution nationale* set in motion by Vichy in the wake of military defeat. Two competing German factions organised propaganda from offices in Paris. Under the ultimate control of Goebbels and the Ministry of Propaganda in Berlin, was the *Propaganda Abteilung*, the section of the *Wehrmacht* in charge of propaganda and censorship in the occupied zone. Vying with them for power was the Ministry of Foreign Affairs, and Ribbentrop's representative in Paris, Otto Abetz.

The policy of collaboration embarked upon by Pétain following his meeting with Hitler at Montoire (October 24th 1940), and the occupation of the north of the country by the Germans, inevitably led to common areas of interest in the social and political affairs of France. Both sides sought to inform and influence public opinion and conduct in areas of mutual concern — one might take the case of *la relève* as an example, a scheme which enabled workers from France to 'replace' French prisoners of war in Germany. Collaboration was re-affirmed by the Paris Protocols of 1941, and Vichy propaganda was to become even more closely aligned to Germany's as Laval tightened his grip on the Vichy government, and as the German troops moved south in 1942 as a result of Allied activity in North Africa. Laval's return to power in April 1942 was to mark the beginning of a number of propaganda campaigns centering on the *Service du travail obligatoire*, the far more draconian successor to *la relève*, and the expulsion of the Jewish community from French society, characterised by the *rafles* carried out in the summer of 1942.

Anti-semitic propaganda did not appear in France for the first time in 1942. A staple of Nazi ideology, the importance of the purity of the German race had been the basis of a series of propaganda campaigns in Germany in 1933, 1935 and 1938. After the Armistice, the Germans sought to alert the French to the threat represented by their own Jewish population and by the *Slav Untermenschen*, both in an effort to further Hitler's plans for increasing European aryanisation, and to prevent the creation of subversive alliances among the disaffected minorities who continued to resist German influence, notably the Communists. The Jews, Freemasons and Bolsheviks were all as frequent targets of Nazi propaganda in France as they were in Germany. The French government and the more right-wing elements in Paris also played on national and ethnic stereotypes and prejudices in their legislation and their propaganda, both in the furtherance of their own agenda for post-Armistice national reconstruction, and in an effort to conform to the wishes of their new political partners. The first *Statut des juifs* was promulgated by Vichy on October 3rd 1940.

German influence also dictated the official attitude in France towards the principal military opponents of the Reich, most notably the English, and subsequently the Russians and the Americans. If border controls were strengthened to prevent Frenchmen from fleeing to London or North Africa, and houses were searched to discover British parachutists that might be sheltering there, such physical measures were backed up by an important propaganda initiative which sought to dissuade the population from ever contemplating such activities. Not only were the major Allied commanders ridiculed in a succession of heavy-handed caricatures, and Russia explicitly branded the source of the dreaded Bolshevism, but, above all, the propagandists emphasised the heavy cost to France of Allied military activities; for example, the destruction caused by successive bombing raids, and operations such as the British attack on the French fleet at Mers-el-Kébir (July, 1940).

In addition to such common concerns, however, both the Germans and the French had their own particular agendas to be addressed through the medium of propaganda. In the wake of the Armistice, for example, the Nazis were keen to promote the integration of their troops in the occupied zone, targeting the younger population with one poster which exhorted the orphaned and homeless to put their faith in the occupying forces. The German army is here personified by a tall and handsome

'Populations abandonnées, faites confiance au soldat allemand!': Poster by T. Matejko, 1940.

soldier of impeccably Aryan extraction, whose broad smile is mirrored by that of the boy he holds in his arms and who is clearly delighted with his new-found friend who can both support and nourish him (see illustration). On the French side, many of the most distinctive propaganda campaigns launched by the Vichy government focused on the essentially domestic issue of the *Révolution nationale* and its leader, *Maréchal* Pétain. Although the *Führerprinzip* is central to Nazi ideology, and there are obvious similarities to be found in the cult of the charismatic leader-figure witnessed in each country, the elevation of Hitler and that of Pétain evolved in parallel to each other, not as part of a concerted propaganda effort. There is no obvious remit apparent on the Germans' part to promote their own leader in France, nor yet to contribute to the overwhelming flood of support for the *Maréchal* that characterises the period from June 1940 to November 1942.

In the furtherance of their political and ideological objectives, all of the agencies involved in influencing public opinion in France had recourse to the younger elements of society, particularly in this earlier period, both as targets of indoctrination, and as the material on which propaganda campaigns were based. For the Vichy government particularly, the importance of the child as propaganda target and ideological icon is fundamental. Here again, parallels between France and Germany are inescapable for the younger generation in Germany played a central role in Nazi thinking, not just in the high-profile Hitler Youth and other semi-military youth movements, but as an integral component of the Reich's *Volksgemeinschaft*. Whatever comparisons one may draw, however, Pétain was not merely aping Nazi Germany by placing much of his hope for the future in the hands of the nation's children; there were many historical, social and ideological reasons why youth should appear such a precious commodity in post-Armistice France. Anyone familiar with the striking poster campaigns which adorned the streets of France in the period 1940-1944 will be aware that one of the key themes promoted by the *Etat français* and its leader, *Maréchal* Pétain, was the importance of the repopulation of France. The First World War had had, as elsewhere in Europe, serious consequences on the country's demographics, and the declining birthrate had been aggravated by economic depression and changing lifestyles in the post-war period. At the beginning of the war, in 1939, the Prime Minister Edouard Daladier had launched a new Family Code which favoured larger families, but this was soon surpassed by the measures taken after the Armistice, which continued to advocate *familles nombreuses*, while placing the Family, and children in particular, in a much broader political and ideological context.

For Vichy France, children represented the Future. Only by repopulating the country could France become great again and assume her rightful position as one of the leading powers in a new, united Europe. At one end of that process of regeneration was the anonymous neonate, the most recent incumbent of the family crib and the subject of so many poster campaigns; a little brother or sister for all the other siblings in the model *famille nombreuse* who coyly present a bouquet of flowers to their mother on the heavily promoted *Fête des mères* (see illustration opposite). At the other end of the scale was the scout, the *compagnon de France*, or any one of the dozens of other skinny teenagers captured by the journalist's camera, proudly posing in a variety of woodland settings. Stripped to the waist, engaged in some physically exacting task like sawing a log, these boys are living up to the moral exhortations of a hundred worthy tracts beginning *Jeunesse de France...* [Youth of France...]. The tiny infant, passive symbol of the rebirth of the nation, will eventually become the active adolescent who is physically able to transform the future, and who, object as well as subject of propaganda, will do so along the lines laid down by Pétain's *Révolution nationale*. But what of the children in

Commissariat Général à la Famille, 'La Journée des Mères, Dimanche 30 Mai 1943': Poster by Phili, 1943.

between - were they to be left to find their own way from cradle to camp fire unaided?

For the historian of Vichy France, the pre-adolescent child features predominantly in the crowd scene, the mass of flag-waving, eager schoolchildren who surround the *Maréchal* as he visits their town or strolls around the streets of Vichy (see illustration overleaf). These children write letters to Pétain expressing their gratitude for his sacrifice, and they buy his portrait to adorn their walls. They follow the precepts of the *Révolution nationale* in their home and school lives, and help the national effort by collecting woollens for charity and killing colorado beetles for the good of the potato crop. Used as a potent image in the propaganda war waged by the *Maréchal's* acolytes and official propagandists, the primary function of the children is to enhance the image created of Pétain the father, the grandfather of the nation, the stern but gentle man endowed with the simplicity, the honesty and the innocence of the youngsters with whom he can communicate so easily; an aging but erect figure, reinvigorated by the enthusiasm and vivacity of those young admirers.

Pétain and schoolchildren: Photo taken during a visit to Paris in 1944. The Maréchal's face is hidden but he is instantly recognisable because of the gloves, the cane and the handshake which which he was associated.

The high-profile use of the pre-adolescent as icon may be important to bolster the image of the *Maréchal*, but for the National Revolution to be a success, the flags have to be waved with conviction. These children have to believe in the future of the New France, and in the vital role that they will play as mothers, farmers, soldiers, etc. Unable, as yet, to participate in the more active roles reserved for the adolescent youth of Vichy France, the young boys and girls of primary school age nevertheless become the targets of a veritable barrage of propaganda to which, in a subtle form of *mise en abîme*, the press photos of flag-waving youngsters would themselves contribute. No opportunity was neglected to win over the affections of the younger members of the population, not just to the cause of National Revolution, but more particularly to the person of the *Maréchal* himself. To this end, many different methods of approach were employed and the visual and plastic arts vied with the written word to ensure that no angle was left uncovered. The deluge of letters and drawings sent by schoolchildren to Pétain at his Vichy hotel testify at least to the short-term success of these initiatives, as do the impressive sums raised by schoolchildren through the sale of Pétain memorabilia, the majority of their customers being themselves of school age.

In comparison with some of the more eye-catching iconography of the Vichy period, children's literature may not immediately attract the attention, a factor that has doubtless contributed to its relative neglect by historians hitherto. Not only have the more innovative methods of propaganda been more appealing to the modern eye, and more accessible to photographic reproduction, but it has perhaps also been assumed that the youngsters of the time would also have been more readily influenced by such visually appealing stimuli. While this may be true in terms of the initial appeal of posters and commemorative artifacts, these media are in fact very limited in terms of the complexity and the penetration of the message they can contain, and their attraction is ultimately short-lived.

In their adoption of the written medium, propagandists were in possession of a number of advantages not enjoyed by the poster artist, or even the manufacturer of the pencil-sharpeners and other gadgets created in the image of the Maréchal or his many totems (kepi, baton, *francisque*,[1] etc.). In children's literature they were appropriating a medium that is already geared towards didacticism as well as entertainment, and where repeated re-reading and a desire for close familiarity and understanding is a fundamental part of the child's interaction with the text. The privileged space created by the storytelling act and the strong, if temporary, bond it fosters between storyteller and audience is one of the greatest attractions of the medium for children and adults alike and an important factor in the transmission of the cultural values such stories many contain. Visual stimulus as well as reinforcement of a message is also provided in children's books through the large number and often lavish quality of the illustrations they contain. Finally, the supreme attraction of the genre for the propagandists of the Vichy régime was the fact that the messages traditionally conveyed to the children of France in

1. The double-bladed war hatchet of the Ancient Franks, symbol of the long heritage of the nation, was adopted as the emblem of the *Etat français*, with the addition of the colours of the national flag to the blades, and the stars of the *Maréchal's* baton to the handle.

their literature bore an uncanny resemblance to the fundamental tenets of the National Revolution, *Travail, Famille and Patrie* - a revolution, therefore, in the true sense of the word. A love of family, the work ethic and one's country were ideals readily accepted on behalf of children before the Second World War, and indeed recur in most children's literature of the nineteenth century. Post 1940 and the fall of France, such desiderata become highly politicised, and inculcating them in the nation's youth is no longer 'education', or 'socialisation', but indoctrination.

There is strong evidence to support the assertion that children's literature in all western cultures has always had at its root a strong socialising imperative.[2] In many tales the didactic element is unblushingly to the fore, witness such genres as the 'cautionary tale', the French *conte moral* (moral tale) etc. Many stories may not proclaim their intention through explicit affiliation to a particular genre, but their title and content make their intention plain — *The History of Little Goody Two-Shoes*, 1765, to which Kramnick devotes some attention, clearly falls into this category.[3] The exemplary nature of such texts is highlighted by the favoured choice of protagonist: anthropophageous, the young reader feeds off the exploits of fictional counterparts, and the experience of one small child becomes a warning to all small children, and in turn, a direct caution to the individual infant engaged in reading the story. In some tales, allegory and hyperbole may dissemble the message behind a veil of fantasy or humour, but the moral or socializing function remains: one does not need the 'moral' appended to the end of Perrault's fairy tale to understand the cautionary angle of *Le Petit chaperon rouge* [Little Red Riding Hood], although some critics have excelled themselves in stretching the symbolic function of this tale to its limits.[4] Even those stories that appear to be pure escapism have, as Stephens ably demonstrates, a vital role to play in reinforcing the image of a stable and acceptable social 'norm', and thus an equally important function in the socialisation process.[5]

Children's literature is thus not only a very valuable reflection of popular culture and social mores but also a significant element in their formation. In a period of political and social stability, which might be defined as being when a consensus exists between the majority of the population and those who govern them, these elements in children's literature will fall into what Ellul characterises as long-term integration propaganda,[6] mirroring the standards and expectations of the dominant social class and the political régime so closely that they are not immediately obvious as propaganda, serving as they do to *reinforce* the status quo. Propaganda becomes overt in times of crisis, when the urgency of the situation necessitates an acceleration of the indoctrination process, to achieve, for example, national unity, and/or to consolidate the position of a new régime whose dominance remains precarious. Here again the process will be far more successful and less easily perceptible if the message transmitted is based in premises already accepted by the target audience, even if expressed in a rather more forceful manner. It should of course be noted, that propaganda is far more easily perceived with the experience of hindsight, particularly when a significant ideological shift has occurred *after* the period under consideration.

2. See, for example, the works of Foulkes, Kramnick, and Stephens, listed in the bibliography.
3. Kramnick, I., 'Children's Literature and Bourgeois Ideology: Observations on Culture and Industrial Capitalism in the Later Eighteenth Century', in Perez Zagorin (ed), *Culture and Politics from Puritanism to the Enlightenment*, Berkeley, 1980, pp. 203-240.
4. See Fromm, E., *The Forgotten Language. An Introduction to the Understanding of Dreams, Fairy Tales and Myths*, Holt, Rinehart and Winston, 1970, and Delarue's criticism of Fromm's analysis, in Delarue, P., 'Les Contes merveilleux de Perrault et la tradition populaire' in *Bulletin Folklorique de l'Ile de France*, Oct-Dec 1951.
5. Stephens, J., *Language and Ideology in Children's Fiction*, Longman, 1992, pp. 122-123.
6. Ellul, J., *Propaganda. The Formation of Men's Attitudes*, Vintage Books, 1973, pp. 74-79 and passim.

La Belle histoire de la France: Vercingétorix, Text by Paluel-Marmont, illustrations by Pierre Luc, Collection 'Lys de France'.

During the Second World War, a high proportion of works continued the task of entertaining the Nation's youth in an essentially unpoliticised form. Many of these stories, such as the *Babar the Elephant* series by Jean de Brunhoff, with their exotic settings and animal protagonists, are essentially what is often termed 'pure escapism', a genre particularly at a premium in times of severe material hardship. While, as we have noted, such stories ultimately reinforce a series of accepted social conventions, however basic these may be, they are not discussed in any detail in this study. Of more immediate relevance are a series of geographical and historical works which, if taken out of context, would not appear to have any particular political significance, but whose aim was to reinforce key themes underpinning Vichy ideology — a good example of the importance of context in pinpointing propaganda. Portraits of key figures in French history were thus designed to highlight the noble ancestry of the race and the importance of strong leadership in times of strife (see illustration opposite). Detailed descriptions of the physical geography of the country provided a means of evoking the great natural wealth and beauty of the country. The practice of presenting France, region by region, was designed to stimulate a love of *la petite patrie*, the small homeland, as a microcosm of, and a forerunner to, national patriotism and a fierce desire to build a new future for *la grande patrie*. Too numerous to list individually, these texts are not discussed in detail in this study, except where an explicit link is established in the text itself with the contemporary situation in which France found herself in the early 1940s.

It is in fact a small but highly-charged group of publications that takes on the task of more overt political indoctrination on behalf of the Germans and the Vichy government. Despite some obvious differences in form (comics, biographies, short stories), and the different agencies behind their production, these works are all linked by a limited set of thematic paradigms, which themselves are all based in stock propaganda topoi used by political régimes all over the world in many different historical and ideological contexts.

The need to unify the nation behind a single vision of the future is vital to any régime seeking to assert its authority,[7] and a number of avenues are available to the propagandist in the furtherance of this aim. An effective means of stimulating cohesion is by putting the image of national solidarity and national identity in jeopardy through the identification or creation of an external aggressor. As recent political leaders have found, war with another nation represents an excellent opportunity to foster patriotic sentiment and to overcome less pressing domestic political and social differences, but this was one option that was not available to Vichy once the Armistice had been signed and the policy of collaboration with Germany embarked upon. The principle, however, held good, and the vicissitudes of the bogey men designated by the *Maréchal* and his followers are well-documented in the many books written since the war about the anti-semitic policy of Vichy France. The legalised persecution that the *statuts des juifs* (October 1940 and June 1941) represented, was accompanied, in the northern zone particularly, by a barrage of propaganda designed to win popular support for a series of measures that began with debarment from certain professions and ended with the wholesale internment and deportation of a very large proportion of the Jewish population in France. Children were used as part of this campaign, both as targets for antisemitic material, and as part of the argument for purging the teaching profession and the children's press, seen as hotbeds of Israelite sedition. Other minority and foreign groups were often associated with the Jews in propaganda aimed at the adult population of France, and the 'Anglo-American-inspired judeo-masonic/bolshevik conspiracy' theory also surfaces in a number of propaganda texts for children in this period. The nature of the themes treated, in conjunction with the violence of the language and illustrations used, marks these texts out as overt propaganda of a particularly unpleasant kind.

In its quest for legitimacy, as well as national stability, the most important task that the Vichy régime set itself was to rekindle in the nation a love of the famous trinity *Travail, Famille, Patrie.* Ellul maintains that overt propaganda can only really succeed when it is building on foundations laid down by long-term integration propaganda. In fixing public attention on the three fundamental tenets of the National Revolution, Vichy was capitalising on the bourgeois socialisation of children that had been in progress since the Revolution of 1789. Also fundamental to Vichy ideology, however, was the conviction that while the moral standards it promoted had previously formed a fundamental part of French life, these high standards had fallen into desuetude in the years between the two wars. This perceived hiatus is central to the ideological thesis of the Vichy propagandists and the literary forms they chose to express it, for it enabled them to create a literature based on the popular propaganda topos of the Fall, and the evocation of a previous Golden Age or Eden which France should strive to recapture.

7. See, for example, Girardet, R., *Mythes et mythologies politiques*, Seuil, 1986, and Ellul, op. cit..

As an essential part of this scenario, and of the closely related issue of Redemption, it was also necessary that Vichy should be able to cast a suitable figure in the role of Saviour of the Nation - a role custom-made for the eighty-four year old *Maréchal* Pétain. The hero of Verdun not only had an unblemished record of devotion to his country, but also the white hair and venerable old age that meant that implicit parallels could be made, not with Jesus the Saviour, but with the Deity himself.

To promote these three fundamental messages among the younger members of the population, the Vichy propagandists had at their disposal a variety of literary genres, from the alphabet primers and history books of the school room, to the comics and story books of the playground, all of which, as we have suggested, already contained a potential for didacticism. In choosing to exploit existing genres in children's literature the régime also benefited from an accelerated access route into the hearts and minds of its young readers. Not only were the different literary forms used easily recognisable, but the recurrence of familiar plot and narrative structures, the use of stereotypes etc. allowed children to absorb more rapidly and easily the introduction of new entities such as the Jew, or *Maréchal* Pétain.

Although a variety of literary approaches were used to indoctrinate the young children of this period, by a number of different agencies and individuals (Section I), one particular theme and narrative style is particularly striking in many of the more literary offerings of the propagandists: that of the fairy story. Looking more closely at this particular paradigm, we turn, in Section II, to two close adaptations of classic '*contes de fées*' (*Le Petit chaperon rouge* [Little Red Riding Hood] and *Barbe-Bleue* [Bluebeard]), which were used to promote anti-semitic and anti-Stalinist propaganda. We then focus on three allegorical accounts of the contemporary French situation, which draw on the fairy tale tradition in both their evocation of a mythical Golden Age, and in their portrayal of the resolution to the conflict (Section III).

In a study of four biographies of Pétain, we then show how the language of fiction, and more particularly of the fairy tale, pervades some ostensibly non-fiction works for children. In the complex relationship between children's fiction and the ideology of Vichy France, life is made to imitate art in a truly symbiotic relationship; for the propagandists' vision of the New France increasingly resembles the fairy tale kingdom of literature. This vision is fed back into literature, and the division between fiction and reality becomes interestingly blurred. While fiction is used as a means of communicating many of the realities of Occupied France, and Little Red Riding Hood teaches children a lesson in antisemitism, reality is exaggerated and perfected in what Girardet refers to as '*ce mystérieux processus d'héroïsation qui aboutit à la transmutation du réel et à son absorption dans l'imaginaire*' [this mysterious process of heroisation which culminates in the transmutation of the real and its absorption into the imaginary].[8] Pétain's life takes on a fairy tale quality suited to his position in that charmed country, '*la France nouvelle*', and his biography begins with those magic words, 'Once upon a time...' (Section IV).[9]

8. Girardet, op. cit., p. 71.
9. Short bibliographical details of all the propaganda texts discussed are given either in the body of the text or in the notes. Full entries, including site code and shelf marks, appear in the Bibliography.

The transmutation of the real, and its absorption into the imaginary, and the opposite process of incorporating the imaginary into a political vision of the country's future, was not restricted to the France inhabited by small children. Fairy-tale France became a popular topos in adult propaganda too while the simple narrative style of children's literature increasingly permeated the prose of the *Maréchal*'s apologists. Youth itself, a fundamental part of Vichy ideology, was held up not only as guarantor of the material future of the country, but also as an ideal in historical and spiritual terms, representing the innocent Golden Age of both the country and the individual. In promoting this vision, and the idealised image of the nation's patriarch, through the language and images of children's literature, the Vichy régime was deliberately placing the adult population in the role of submissive children, and children's literature was thus used not only to indoctrinate the nation's youth, but also to infantilise its adults.

I
Children's Literature in France, 1940–1944

The effects of the war on children's publishing

On the eve of the Second World War children's literature was flourishing. Renonciat estimates that a total of approximately 300 authors and illustrators were writing for children at this time, producing a total of some 500 titles annually, with around 40 publishers active in the field.[1] Many of these editors, such as Bourrelier & Cie, Delagrave, and the larger companies such as Nathan or Mame, started off producing school books or *livres de prix* and only subsequently moved into leisure publishing. While it is possible to assess with some degree of accuracy the state of children's publishing in the late 1930s, however, it is far more difficult to ascertain the level of production during the Second World War. Not only have company records been destroyed, but the official bibliographies of the period such as the *Bibliographie de la France* provide only an incomplete picture, often failing to distinguish children's books from general literary production.

Figures that have survived concerning the production of children's books during the First World War show that numbers more than halved from 1912 to 1914, and then halved again in 1915. After that sudden and dramatic fall, production continued at a much decreased level throughout the rest of the war.[2] Even without definitive figures to back up the assertion, it is inevitable that a similar decline would have occurred during the Second World War. In both wars, material restrictions, problems of distribution, and shortages of manpower were major factors in restricting the book trade, and such problems were exacerbated in the Second World War by the physical occupation of a substantial and strategic portion of the territory. Companies remaining in operation in Paris after the Occupation risked being requisitioned (Hachette), bombed (Mame) or falling victim to the Germans' policy of aryanisation (Calmann-Levy, Offenstadt, Nathan, etc.). For many companies publishing books for children in the capital, the disruption of enforced flight from Paris was followed, on their return, by an equally disruptive and restrictive régime of censorship, where the age of the intended audience for their publications attracted no particular dispensations or favours from the Germans. Literary activity was further stifled in less obvious but equally efficient ways; the attribution of the 'prix jeunesse' by the publishing house Editions Bourrelier & Cie., for example, first awarded in 1935, was suspended for the duration of the war.

The experience of many children's comics appears typical of the relative position of children's publishing in the northern and southern zones between 1940 and 1944. The banning of American comics from

1. Renonciat, A., *Livre mon ami: lectures enfantines 1914-54. (Catalogue établi et rédigé par Annie Renonciat),* Mairie de Paris, 1991, p. 69.
2. Renonciat gives the following figures from the *Catalogue général de la librairie française of Otto Lorenz* : 69 titles in 1915, 40 in 1916, 38 in 1917, 39 in 1918. This is opposed to 144 titles published in 1914, 190 in 1913 and 331 in 1912 (Renonciat, op. cit., p. 11).

December 1941 when the Americans entered the war, the aryanisation of companies such as Montsouris and Offenstadt, and the ever-worsening problem of paper shortages, meant that 10 comics, the vast majority of those produced in the northern zone, disappeared between January and March 1942. Rare exceptions were the Breton publication *O Lo Lê* which survived almost until the end of the war (15 November 1940 - 15 May 1944), the very brief appearance of *Etc...* (Paris, 3 December 1942 - 3 January 1943), and the only new comic to be launched in Paris with any success, *Le Téméraire* (15 January 1943 - 1 August 1944). Those companies that withdrew to the southern zone in 1940, or which had always operated in regional centres such as Lyons, Marseilles and Nice, experienced a very different fate to their northern colleagues. Although a comic like *Tarzan* was forced to close in 1941 because of its American connections, some 15 other titles were produced in the south between 1940 and 1944, 12 of these lasting well into 1944. The south was not, however, untouched by the material restrictions that hampered publishing in the north. Print-runs were limited, some issues had to be abandoned completely, and all were forced to move to a reduced format, particularly after the Germans moved south in November 1942.[3]

The War in Children's Literature

In the absence of dependable statistics concerning global production of children's literature during the war, determining the relative output of propaganda is thus particularly hazardous, and all the more so as propaganda texts are today scattered among a number of public collections,[4] and may also exist, perhaps unrecognised or forgotten, in private hands. Texts that have not physically survived to the present day will not necessarily feature in bibliographies of the period, and may therefore have disappeared without trace. The process of occultation may be furthered by the complicity of authors themselves, not unwilling for their war-time *écrits* to sink into oblivion. From the figures that can be deduced from a collation of various sources, however, it would appear that out-and-out propaganda books formed a relatively small proportion of the total output of children's literature during the Second World War. The majority of books continued to provide unpoliticised escapism through the anthropomorphic adventures of a variety of animals, and a liberal helping of fairy tales and '*robinsonades*'. Doubtless such texts play their habitual role in the socialisation process as referred to in the introduction, but the social norm that they portray is so essentially similar to that portrayed before the war, that they cannot be said to play any role in the propaganda campaign.

To give some idea of the possible figures involved in the output of overt propaganda, the 1941 edition of the *Bibliographie de la France* announced some 80 new books for children (not including *estampes* [prints]). Of these, only three directly mentioned the *Maréchal* in their title.[5] From the titles alone, only 3 other works appear to have any relevance to the current study. One can only guess at the exact nature of a book entitled *La Périlleuse mission du Capitaine Jerry*, by Giraud, (Paris, Gautier

3. For further details see Gervereau, L, 'La Presse enfantine' in Gervereau, L., and Peschanski, D., (eds), *La Propagande sous Vichy 1940-44*, Collection Publications de la BDIC, 1990, pp. 180-187.
4. Most notable among these are the collections of the Bibliothèque de la Documentation Contemporaine at Nanterre, the Bibliothèque Municipale in Vichy, the Centre de Documentation Juive Contemporaine, Paris and the Bibliothèque "*L'Heure joyeuse*", Paris.
5. Paluel-Marmont, A., *Il était une fois un Maréchal de France*, les Editions et Publications Françaises [1941], and Hérault, P., *La Vie d'honneur du Maréchal Pétain racontée et illustrée pour les jeunes français*, Farré et Freulon [1940] (both discussed in Section IV below), and Chancerel, L., *Oui Monsieur le Maréchal*, Arthaud, a picture book for children.

Languereau, 1940), but the patriotic message of a text entitled *Vive la France* (Pierre Jalabert) seems clear. Of contemporary interest, if not directly political, was a cut-out book of warships.

In the lists produced in 1942, some 90 children's books are referred to, and somewhat surprisingly, none of the titles immediately suggests propaganda. Further investigation of the most promising titles still available confirms that none of the works themselves is overtly political, although some essentially anodine books were not completely untouched by the *Révolution nationale* and the desire to spread its message. Such an example is the story of a tea-party recounted in Crassé-Sceillier's *Un jour de fête*, (Editions 'Alsatia', Paris, 1942), which in its introduction, reminded the little girls of their future duty to reverse the trend of falling birthrates.[6]

As the *Révolution nationale* faltered, and Pétain's political influence declined, so we see an increase in the number of propaganda texts produced, according to the titles listed in the *Bibliographie de la France*. Although details of children's books were given only for the first 6 months of 1943, and some of those listed were actually published in the latter months of 1942, of the 42 works listed, seven stand out as being part of the Vichy propaganda effort, some concentrating particularly on the *Maréchal* himself.[7] The increasingly German orientation of much of the propaganda in France from 1943 onwards is demonstrated by the appearance of the fascist-orientated comic-book, *Le Téméraire*, whose first volume appeared on January 15th 1943.[8]

From the evidence of surviving collections, the early months of 1944 did not prove conducive to the publication of pro-Vichy propaganda. Not only were material shortages at their peak at this time, but the political situation was in a continual state of flux as the fortunes of the Allies continued to improve. In fact this period saw the beginnings of a counter-attack by writers working on behalf of Free France and even the Resistance (as well, perhaps, as on their own account), and the Liberation of June 1944 was followed quite rapidly by the publication of a number of stories for children apparently elaborated in the final months of the Occupation. Among the most notable of these are a comic book produced by the Auvergne resistance movement, the *Corbeau déchaîné*, and a comic-strip presentation of the war, entitled *La Bête est morte. La guerre mondiale chez les animaux* written by a former apologist of the Vichy régime (see Section III).[9]

7. See the works of Chéronnet, Paluel-Marmont, Pellos and Reynaud listed in the Bibliography, plus the anonymous text *Vercingétorix, la belle histoire de la France*.
8. For a detailed analysis of this twice-monthly comic, subtitled '*Le journal de la jeunesse moderne*' ['the comic of today's youth'], see Ory, P., *Le Petit Nazi illustré. Le Téméraire (1943-1944)*, Editions Albatros, 1979.
9. For details of these and other Liberation texts for children, see Proud, J., 'Plus ça change...? Propaganda fiction for children in France 1940-1945' in the proceedings of the conference *Liberation, Image and Event (Sussex, 1994)*, Berg, 1995.

6. Pardonnez-moi si j'ose/Mes chers petits enfants,/Vous parler d'autres choses/Que de vos jeux charmants.../Mais de ces images et histoires de votre âge il faudra tirer une conclusion utile. C'est que vous, petites filles très chères, vous vous préparez au plus beau et plus béni des métiers, celui de "MAMANS"....
[Forgive me if I dare/My dear little children,/To speak to you of other things/Than your charming games/But from these pictures and stories written for you, you must glean a useful message. That is that you, darling little girls, you are preparing yourselves for the most beautiful and the most blessed of professions, that of being "MOTHERS"...].
A similar theme is found in Merlin's L'Alphabet de la famille, (Paris, 1944) based on radio programme produced by the Commissariat Général à la Famille. This gave the letter M as 'M comme maman' (M for Mother) with the detail 'Et Françoise en berçant ses poupées leur chante son joli rêve: être maman'. [And Françoise while rocking her dolls, sings to them of her beautiful dream: to be a mother]

While the picture presented by the *Bibliographie de la France* is certainly incomplete, it nevertheless suggests that quite a high proportion of books produced during the Second World War were not concerned with the propaganda effort of the Vichy régime, nor with that of the German occupant or indeed with the war in any form. This is in direct contrast to the First World War, when children's publishing was mobilised on a huge scale on behalf of the war effort, the war providing both the setting and the subject-matter for the vast majority of new publications.[10] One of the reasons for this disparity is the very different position in which France found herself in 1940 compared with 1914-18.

In the First World War, a clear and unchanging enemy could be distinguished throughout a conflict in which alliances also remained relatively stable. The mobilisation of public opinion against the Germans was further aided by the fact that they were a traditional enemy of France, the position of Alsace and Lorraine remaining as a painful reminder of their most recent armed exchanges. Long association breeds caricatures and stereotypes, and anti-German propaganda in the First World War, for both adults and children alike, was aided by the established figure of the *Boche* — an instantly recognisable literary and visual stereotype which perhaps remained particularly effective throughout the war as a result of the absence of any real contact between the majority of the civilian population and the enemy forces.

The situation in the Second World War was clearly more complex. The Phoney War, with its emphasis on the defence of Poland and of Finland did not provide the same galvanising effect that a direct invasion of France would have done. Many Frenchmen were either confused as to the exact reasons why France should be involved in such a conflict, or disgruntled that they should be called away from more pressing duties, particularly on the farms, when their own property was not apparently under any direct threat. From the outbreak of war, through Dunkirk, the Armistice, Montoire, Mers-el-Kébir etc., the official position of France went through a whirling kaleidoscope of changing affiliations and conflicting allegiances. Not only was France's relationship with Germany to change radically with the signing of the Armistice and the agreement of a policy of collaboration, but her attitude to Britain and Russia was also to undergo a series of dramatic U-turns. The French Communists had problems of their own, keeping up with the changing alliances that Stalin entered into, from the Russo-German Pact of 1939 to his entry into the war on the side of the Allies in 1941.

The reaction of the populace to such a contradictory series of transformations was further complicated by the unusual partition of the country into the northern and southern zones. People forced to flee their homes in the north, and those who remained in towns occupied in 1940 clearly had a different experience of the Germans than the populations living in the south, although their turn soon came to meet the invader at closer quarters. Paris still remained a focal point for cultural activity, and the administrative centre for the occupying forces, but it was no longer the capital of the nation, the government now residing in the many hotels offered by the spa town of Vichy. The broadcasts of de

10. See Renonciat, op. cit., pp. 9-21.

Gaulle, and the incursions of the Resistance served only to fragment the popular perception of the war and of national identity further. Even within Vichy itself, conflict over policies and presentation bubbled just below the surface, often erupting into overt wrangling, most noticeably with the 'resignation' of Laval in December 1940.

While patriotic fervour encouraged every children's author in the First World War to take up the pen for the national cause, that element of national consensus was undoubtedly lacking in 1940. The amount of 'escapist' literature to be produced for children during this period tends furthermore to suggest that, on the contrary, a desire to avoid any evocation of the contemporary situation was uppermost in the minds of authors and readers alike, forced into too close a contact with the realities of war in their everyday lives, through the Occupation, the absence of loved ones in prison camps in Germany, and the economic and nutritional deprivations experienced in every part of the country.

If the number of overt propaganda texts for children promoting the ideology of the Vichy régime produced during this period is relatively small, dissenting voices are apparently non-existent. Although a number of pro-Resistance, and pro-de Gaulle stories for children appeared very soon after the Liberation, the system of censorship operated by both the Vichy government and the German authorities between 1940 and June 1944 ensured that anti-German or anti-Vichy texts were very unlikely to appear during that time. All manuscripts were liable to inspection before publication, official visas were granted only to acceptable works (illustrations were subject to a separate visa), and the judicious distribution of paper served as an effective form either of encouragement or dissuasion by the authorities. Existing texts for children were also subject to the censor's scrutiny, but while a number of children's books did appear on the second *Liste Otto* of July 8th 1942, their content could hardly be considered subversive. Of the works censored, the majority were school books dating from the 1920s (see below), and the remainder were essentially composed of English translations and works by Jewish authors, expunged because of the nationality of their author regardless of actual content.

Propaganda and Pedagogy

Pupils of primary school age were eased into the precepts of the *Révolution nationale* through the visual arts, which were not merely seen as a suitable vehicle for reproducing infinite portraits of Pétain, but also as an important pedagogical tool. As the Ministry of Education decreed in 1942, the two functions of propaganda and pedagogy could be very happily combined by decorating classrooms with suitably patriotic images designed to inspire emulation in the young pupils' hearts. In response to the Ministry's wishes, the *Information de l'Etat Français* published a series of 'documents' between October and December 1942 entitled *La France que nous aimons* 'destined for the decoration of the classroom'.[11] Active participation in the iconographic boom was further encouraged by the provision of colouring books such as that which portrayed the

11. This series introduced the pupils to the most illustrious Frenchmen (and two women) from Vercingétorix to Pétain. They are: Vercingétorix, Clovis, Ste Geneviève, Martel, St Louis, Jeanne d'Arc, Bayard, Jacques Cartier, Henri IV, Sully, Richelieu, Turenne, La Fontaine, Pascal, Louis XIV, Denis Papin, Jean Bart, Cugnot, Les Frères Montgolfier, Marceau, Napoléon, Surcouf, Bugeaud, Pasteur, Ader-Blériot-Mermoz, Branly, le Père de Foucauld, Guynemer, Pétain.

travels of the *Maréchal*, entitled *Présentez armes!*[12] and cut-out books such as the inspirationally-titled *Maréchal Pétain, Chef de l'Etat français*[13] For lighter, if still edifying, relief, patriotic songs and games were also provided. The propaganda value of the latter did not necessarily end with their subject matter, however, as illustrated by the *Jeu du drapeau*, a game presented as the prize for the best drawings submitted during the propaganda campaign '*La France que nous aimons*'.[14]

The pedagogic process and learning needs of the very young pupils were further capitalised on by the Vichy propagandists through the introduction of highly politicised *abécédaires* such as that edited by the Bureau de Documentation du Chef d'Etat in 1943, which featured the *Maréchal* himself or something closely connected with him (kepi, baton etc.), on every page. At a slightly more advanced level were simple texts such as *Les Trois leçons de Lududu, maître d'école*, the three lessons, of course, being: *Travail, Famille* and *Patrie.*[15]

Despite the almost overwhelming attractions of the visual medium, however, the propagandists of Vichy France were not blind to the possibilities of the written word, even for a target audience of primary school age. While the government very actively promoted the introduction of visual propaganda material into the classroom, however, the relationship between text-based propaganda and the school curriculum is somewhat more ambiguous. If many of the texts discussed below were clearly akin to those used in the schoolroom through the kind of reading activity they promoted, through certain elements of content and presentation, and the didactic purpose common to education and indoctrination, it would not appear that they were either commissioned or adopted for use as part of the established curriculum. The traditional elements of the primary school curriculum (history, geography, French language) and the official texts used to teach them, appear to have remained practically unchanged throughout the war. A certain number of history and reading texts were banned, and others were judicially pruned where they contained unflattering references to barbaric Hunnish hordes,[16] but no new Vichy-orientated works were introduced into these areas of the school syllabus, not least because of internal wranglings between the different parties involved in proposed modifications, and the more material problems associated with paper shortages.

If these subject-areas, officially at least, experienced propaganda by omission rather than commission, this was not the case in another small section of the curriculum — *Education morale, civique et patriotique.* Taking up only one hour a week of the 30 compulsory hours of the *cours préparatoire, élémentaire,* and *moyen* (see Appendix 1), this class represented the most explicit exposure that students received to the tenets of the *Révolution nationale* if we discount the classes in physical education and practical hygiene that also featured on the syllabus. While no texts were specifically named to accompany this course save the '*messages du Maréchal Pétain*', many of the propaganda texts which promoted *Travail, Famille and Patrie* would certainly have been highly suitable for it, as the course description reads very much like a synopsis of a number of these texts

12 Cosmos, n.d., Autorisation Vichy OA 245.

13 Office central de l'imagerie, 1941, Accord de la censure no. OA 237.

14 Vichy, Wallon Ed CPRN [1943].

15 *Les Trois leçons de Lududu, maître d'école*, text by Léon Chancerel, illustrations by André Paul, Paris, Grenoble, La Gerbe de France, n.d..

16 *Archives Nationales*, Paris, AJ ^{40} 559 and AJ ^{40} 560 '*Censure des livres et des films scolaires: correspondance avec les maisons d'édition*'.

(see Appendix 1). The absence of any reference to this particular course in the publications themselves, however, would appear to confirm that they were not officially commissioned, nor primarily destined, for such a function.

Further debate over the relationship between propaganda and the classroom may arise from the fact that many items of 'literary' propaganda for children were produced under the auspices of government ministries, or by organisations closely associated with the régime. One of the most notable features of the *Etat français* is the large number of organisations that were quickly created, or adapted from existing groups, to ensure that the physical and ideological education of the nation's youth proceeded along suitable lines after the Armistice of 1940. On the one hand, there were the government ministries of Youth and of Education, with three successive ministers in the latter state office commissioning a series of studies of primary and secondary education in the period 1940–44. On the other, there were the many catholic-orientated scouting movements and other youth camps described in detail by Halls designed to give the adolescent population of France their first introduction to the physical and moral commitments of a disciplined semi-military lifestyle. In addition to these organisations specifically orientated towards the younger section of the population, there were the propaganda offices of both Germany and Vichy France, which targeted children as part of their much broader remit to influence the thinking and behaviour of the nation as a whole. The Vichy government was particularly keen to promote and maintain the incredible popularity of its leader, Philippe Pétain, in whom its authority and influence over the people of France essentially rested. Hence we see the creation of offices such as the *Bureau de Documentation du Chef d'Etat*, and above all, the *Imagerie du Maréchal*, whose sole object was to come up with a succession of artifacts, pictures and documentation featuring Pétain's likeness or the symbolic emblems of his personal qualities or favoured doctrine.

The *Imagerie du Maréchal* was responsible for many of the more visually-orientated propaganda texts that appeared during this period, such as Louis Chéronnet's educational paean to the rural work ethic, *Les Artisans de la ville et du village*, (1943). The propaganda office, the *Information de l'Etat Français*, produced the series of pictures entitled *La France que nous aimons* referred to above, destined for the decoration of school classrooms, while the *Bureau de Documentation du Chef d'Etat* produced a number of more text-orientated publications such as Dancette's *Il était une fois un pays heureux*, [1943], discussed in Section III, and *De Vercingétorix à Pétain. Le Don de soi-même*, (text by Jacques Reynaud, Illustrations by Jean Chièze, 1942) whose title gives a clear indication of the message of the book.

If none of the texts which form the corpus of this study was part of the official school syllabus, although some were certainly produced under the auspices of government-related organisations, this is not to say that schools did not play an important role in the circulation of literary propaganda in the Vichy régime. The *Librairie du Maréchal* in the rue Gay-Lussac in Paris sold schoolbooks at reduced prices, and introduced its young clients to a range of other 'suitable' material. School libraries could also be counted on as a source of improving literature, and the schoolyard provided a popular forum for swapping and discussing the latest books and comics. Schools also played a central role in many of the charitable enterprises that relied on children for support. Teachers helped organise the collection of woollens for prisoners of war after school, trips to the potato fields to rid the plants of colorado beetles, and the sale of patriotic '*brochures*', many of which were themselves aimed at the younger population.[17]

Children's Propaganda: Principal Genres

Exemplary lives

The Ministry of Education may not have been directly responsible for the publication of the majority of propaganda texts published under Vichy, but many works extolling the virtues of Philippe Pétain are very closely related to the history and reading books and the exemplary lives used on the traditional syllabus. These texts establish Pétain's *bona fides* by placing him at the culmination of a series of national heroes that starts with Vercingétorix, and passes through such noble luminaries as Bayard, Joan of Arc and Henry IV.[18] The Maid of Orleans had of course always been a popular subject of devotion in France, and children had long been encouraged to worship at her altar. In adult literature and theatre she was to prove an ambiguous icon during the Occupation. For many she symbolised the traditional rivalry between France and England, an important propaganda theme after the British sinking of the French fleet at Mers-el-Kébir. For others, however, she embodied the spirit of patriotic defiance against *any* foreign encroachment on French soil, and the very antithesis of the Vichy policy of collaboration. In children's literature, there is no such dichotomy; Joan is enlisted firmly on the side of the Maréchal. In an anonymous and undated work entitled *Jeanne d'Arc. Sa mission, son exemple*, published by the *Secrétariat Général de l'Information*, a direct line of affiliation is established between her heroic deeds and those of Philippe Pétain: '*... si les moyens diffèrent, avec Pétain comme avec Jeanne, le combat reste identique*' [... if the means differ, with Pétain, as with Joan, the battle remains the same].[19] Not only does this book serve to emphasise the notion of the *Patrie* (which presumably Pétain has saved by negotiating the best possible terms in the Armistice), it also elevates Pétain, by association with Joan, to the level of sainthood. Above all, it also provides a direct link between its subject and its target audience; implicitly through its recounting of the actions of a young heroine, explicitly in the conclusion of the story:

> *A ce travail, [la régénération de la France], le peuple de France doit se donner tout entier. Mais, comme au temps de Jeanne, il a besoin pour se réveiller, d'un actif ferment de jeunesse.*
>
> To this task [the regeneration of France], the people of France must give themselves entirely. But, as in Joan's time, in order to bestir themselves, they need the active leaven of youth.[20]

17 From October 1940, the *Secours national*, under the direction of R. Garric based in Gannat (just outside Vichy), coordinated the actions of a number of private charities. School children were an integral part of the activities of this organisation.

18 See, for example, Reynaud, J., op. cit. and Anon, *Vercingétorix, la belle histoire de la France*, Illustrations by Pierre Luc, Paris, Editions artistiques et littéraires, 1943.

19 Anon, *Jeanne D'Arc. Sa mission, son exemple*, Secrétariat Général de l'Information, n.d..

20 op. cit..

Idealised Biography

The exemplary lives referred to above, and other texts glorifying the artisanal idyll, and the contribution of the French colonies,[21] though essentially non-fiction, all show the early-warning signs of the 'heroisation' process described by Girardet and referred to in the Introduction. This process is seen in a much more advanced stage in the hagiographic biographies of Pétain, discussed in Section IV, which adopt a number of elements characteristic of the fairy tale in their portrayal of the *Maréchal*'s childhood and his rise to national preeminence.

Comic Books and Adventure Stories

The comic book was particularly well-suited to the patriotic tenor of the *Révolution nationale*, for many of the comics already in existence in 1940 had sprung from nationalist tendencies aroused before the war by the increasing invasion of American comic books and characters (Mickey Mouse, Tarzan, etc.). This invasion had led to the creation of a number of very ostentatiously French comics, with titles such as *Bayard* and *Francis*, which were at pains to stress the entirely French nature of their authorship and production.[22] Established comics, such as *Benjamin*, founded in 1929 and subtitled '*journal intégralement français*' found themselves in a very favourable position at the Armistice, and were to continue during the war period with very little change, except for relocation in the southern zone, and frequent quotations from and references to *Maréchal* Pétain. New patriotic comics were also created during the war, most notably *Le Téméraire* founded in 1943 (see above).

In the First World War, the adventure book had been one of the most popular literary genres for children, a format particularly suited to the clear-cut relationship between France and Germany, where nothing was more natural than for young French protagonists to stumble across and ultimately foil a series of fiendish plots cunningly laid by fifth columnists working for the beastly *Boche*. In the Second World War, such 'real-life' adventure stories are virtually non-existent, their composition and publication being necessarily limited to the early months of the conflict. A rare exception is *La Mort d'Eric* by Serge Dalens [Yves de Verdilhac], one of a series of stories featuring a group of boys, headed by the eponymous hero of this volume. In this, the fourth of the series, Eric and his chums have reached the required age to fight for their country, which they proceed to do in a number of the most famous encounters of the early months of the war, including Dunkirk.[23] Direct references to contemporary events only resurface in children's literature generally at the end of the war when, after the Liberation, the recent activities of the Resistance movement began to feature in children's literature (see for example, Paul Vincent's *La Belle aventure du Disque Rouge*, Paris, 1945).

The adventure story survived in the strip cartoons and short stories of the comics of 1940–44, but devoid of any direct reference to contemporary events. Among the valiant heroes and arch villains that people their pages, however, the alert reader will soon appreciate the preponderance of blond warriors and princes who are called upon to pit their wits and superior muscle power against the evil machinations of a variety of scientists, space aliens etc., who with their dark hair and hooked noses all bear an uncanny stereotypical resemblance to those other undesirable aliens, the Jews, Bolsheviks and Freemasons.

21 See, for example, Piquet, V., *L'Empire Français et les pionniers*, Illustrations by Henri Dimpre, la Publicité Synchronisée, Paris, Editions CPRN, n.d.. Topics covered: Les Précurseurs - les croisés, les Bourgeois de Vaisseaux, l'Inde, L'Ile Dauphine, l'Ile Bourbon, L'Ile de France, le Canada, Les Antilles, l'Eldorado, l'Algérie, Le Maroc, l'Afrique Noire, Madagascar, L'Indo-Chine.

22 For further details of these and other nationalist books produced in the inter-war period, see Renonciat, op. cit., pp. 85-88.

23 Although it was written in 1940, *La Mort d'Eric* was first published in 1942 with permission, and only a few cuts, from the German censor. Recent re-editions of this and the other volumes in the series by Safari, Signes de Piste, contain details provided by Dalens himself of the conditions surrounding the publication of his work during the War.

Fairy-tale France

Comic books were not the only medium through which the short story reached the young reading public in France; many appeared as independent publications, usually in quite a large format, copiously illustrated in colour. Of these works, a small proportion may be considered overt propaganda, and the most striking characteristic to link them all is a marked emphasis on the narrative techniques and thematic content of the fairy tale. Of these publications, the closest parodies of the classic fairy tale are to be found in a violent anti-semitic tale based on the story of *Little Red Riding Hood*, and an attack on Stalinist Russia along the lines of another Perrault classic, *Bluebeard*. It is with these two stories that we begin our more detailed analysis of the fairy tale theme in Vichy propaganda.

II
Perrault, Pétain, and the politicisation of the Fairy Tale

The enemies of Vichy France

The role of antisemitism in Nazi ideology is well documented, and its influence in Vichy France scarcely less so, even if historians remain undecided as to the exact apportionment of blame. Grey areas may remain as to direct responsibility for the *Statuts juifs* promulgated by Vichy, and statistics concerning the deportation of French nationals and non-French Jews may continue to be debated, but evidence of an antisemitic policy in Vichy France cannot be denied. Just as the underlying tenets of the *Révolution nationale* were familiar to the French nation before Pétain brought them to particular preeminence, so antisemitism was a trait which already existed in the national character prior to the Second World War. This existing current of antisemitism among adults is important in explaining the choice of the Jews as a target for agitation propaganda in Vichy France, and also has consequences for the formal considerations associated with the choice of literary medium through which that message was to be transmitted to the younger generation.

As a result of the peculiar circumstances in which France found herself after the Armistice, the role of designated enemy, a fundamental prerequisite for national unity in the eyes of the propagandist, was apparently vacant. If the Germans could not form the basis of the kind of agitation propaganda featuring the *Boche* that characterised the First World War, other candidates were not lacking; indeed, the very profusion of possible targets necessitated their amalgamation into one composite enemy. In this way, the energies of propagandist and propagandee alike could be channelled into one major effort, avoiding diffusion and dilution, while further fuel was added to the conspiracy theory so necessary to create the conditioned reflex that throws a nation's people into each other's arms, and into the thrall of the régime that promises to protect against the perceived threat. All of the chosen subjects of Vichy paranoia, English, Freemasons, Jews and Bolsheviks, were traditional enemies of the Nation - only the Americans were regarded with a certain degree of ambivalence prior to their alliance with England in the War, not least because of their historic opposition to the British in 1776.

As a corollary to his belief that it is effectively impossible to persuade a group to act in a manner, or to believe a proposition, that is diametrically opposed to its normal behaviour patterns/beliefs, Ellul maintains that agitation propaganda will only work if the ground has already been carefully prepared through a long process of social conditioning.[1] The history of antisemitism in France, therefore, designated the Jew as an ideal target for a campaign that sought to demonise a distinct section of the community and to lay at its door direct responsibility for the crushing defeat suffered by France in 1940. Traditionally associated with the Jew was the Freemason, '*la fille du judaïsme*'

1. Ellul, op. cit., p. 15 and passim.

[the daughter of Judaism][2] and this coupling was stressed in much of the non-fiction propaganda concerning children in the Second World War, which sought to portray innocent youth in the clutches of an education system dominated by the Hebrew nation and the Masonic Lodge (cf *La Fausse éducation nationale. L'Emprise judéo-maçonnique sur l'école française*, by Jean Bertrand [Henry Babize] and Claude Wacogne, CAD, n.d.

The organisation that published or coordinated much of the antisemitic and antimasonic propaganda in France, the *Centre d'Action et de Documentation anti-maçonnique* (CAD),[3] and its co-founder and director, Henri Coston, believed that children were the targets of Jewish/Masonic influence not just in the schoolroom, but also in their homes, through the literature they chose to read in their spare time, most notably comic books. This was the inspiration behind a booklet entitled *Les Corrupteurs de la jeunesse. La main-mise Judéo-maçonnique sur la presse enfantine*, written by Coston himself.[4] This text reiterated the threat represented by schools, enlarged the scope to cover a number of youth movements, but concentrated above all on the pernicious effects of comic books such as the 'Masonic' *Les Petits bonshommes*. In a further demonstration of the propagandist's economy and art, Coston also attacked *Copain-Cop* and *Mon Camarade*, two comics supposedly composed by scions of '*le Jérusalem moscovite*', the editor being not only a Freemason, but also a Communist! Some spin-offs of *Mon Camarade* were said by Coston to be translations of Soviet publications, and the Bolshevik connection is stressed on the cover of the booklet, which gives prominence to a grasping taloned hand, the traditional image used by Vichy and Nazi propagandists alike to evoke the peril from the East.

With their entry into the war in December 1941, the ambivalent status of the Americans was instantly resolved, and the propagandists were quick to include them in the opprobrium heaped on the other enemies of the régime. With Judaism and Masonry still as fundamental ingredients, the Americans were added to the melting pot of accusation and conspiracy bubbling around the corrupters of French youth. Coston accused 'le trust judéo-yankee' of being behind such publications as the *Journal de Mickey*, brainchild of the Mason Disney, and the publisher Winckler, a Jew and a Freemason.[5]

Coston accused the Jews and Freemasons, not to mention the Communists, of setting out to win new adepts, of demoralising French youth, and of slowly fermenting a process of disaffection for the homeland which had culminated in the young adults of the 40s being unwilling to participate in the '*tâches grandioses que lui offre la Révolution nationale*' [the great tasks offered to them by the National Revolution]. Accusations were not always so clearly stated. 'Corruption' is a charge frequently levelled against these forces, an emphasis on the lubricious nature of the Jew suggesting that moral, if not physical, corruption was particularly feared. In *Les Corrupteurs de la jeunesse*, apart from labelling the Jewish publisher Offenstadt '*un abject pornographe*' [an abject pornographer],[6] Coston accuses the comics he attacks of provoking hatred in the heart of their readers ('[*de*] *susciter la haine au coeur de leurs jeunes lecteurs*'),[7] but what the concrete result of this hatred might be is not specified. The question of what these forces were supposed to be doing to the children is all the more interesting when we consider that one of the means used to counteract this propaganda was for Vichy, in turn, to

2. Coston, H. *Les Corrupteurs de la jeunesse. Main-mise judéo-maçonnique sur la presse enfantine, Bulletin d'information, numéro spécial anti-maçonnique*, Paris [?1941/2], p. 12.
3. Founded in 1941 by Henri Coston and Paul Lafitte, the Centre was housed in the rue Puteaux in Paris, in the former premises of the *Grande Loge de France*.
4. The date of this publication is difficult to determine, the BDIC catalogue suggests 1941/2, Agathon gives 1943.
5. Coston, op. cit., pp. 23-24.
6. Idem, p. 18.
7. Idem, p. 16.

direct agitation propaganda at the children themselves, not just to the adult readers of texts such as those produced by the CAD. What did the Vichy propagandists seek to achieve in fostering antisemitism among its young audience?

This question is not fully answered by an analysis of the texts themselves, but such propaganda seems to have been primarily aimed at inducing the children to shun the Jewish population, and more generally to reinforce the sentiment of antisemitism abroad in the country, perhaps with the intention of causing the children to accept, even to applaud, the removal of a substantial proportion of the Jewish population from their immediate vicinity. While there is no suggestion of charging the infant readers of such texts with complicity in the fate that ultimately awaited Jewish deportees, and indeed the final destination of these victims was never openly avowed by the Vichy régime, the extreme violence latent in the two anti-semitic texts studied below, and in all the anti-enemy propaganda for children investigated, has disturbing reverberations for those familiar with the genocidal aspirations of the Nazi régime.

Origin of Vichy Texts

The reference to Nazi Germany raises the important question of the exact source of this agitation propaganda. If the *Révolution nationale* had similarities with Nazi ideology, not least in its insistence on the importance of clean-limbed youth to the future of the nation and a new Europe, the enemies chosen by the régime to unite the people were very much the enemies of the Third Reich. Unlike some of the improving works referred to in Section I that were produced by government organisations, the anti-enemy propaganda for children that has survived to this day is not explicitly linked to any particular Vichy ministry, but rather appears to be the work of a small number of publishers based in Paris. Their origin in the Occupied Zone is significant, tying in with the essentially Nazi nature not only of the message they were transmitting, but also with the choice of agitation propaganda as a medium. This is a medium, particularly where oratory is concerned, used far more readily by the extremist elements in French politics, such as Doriot or the *Légion*.

A prolific source of anti-enemy works for children was the publisher NEF, whose initials or whose logo of a fully-rigged galleon appears on two antisemitic works to have survived: *Youpino*, and *Doulce France et Grojuif* [Sweet France and Fatjew] (see illustration overleaf). The former is undated and anonymous, while the latter is signed 'N', has illustrations by 'JB' and was published in 1942. According to Rossignol,[8] this publisher is not to be confused with the *Nouvelles Editions Françaises*, the new name given by Robert Denoël in November 1940 to a company originally founded in 1937, which he used to bring out his collection '*Les Juifs en France*'. Despite this similarity of interests, NEF is identified by Rossignol[9] as being the *Nouvelles Etudes Françaises* (7 rue Darboy, Paris) which published a number of works, usually undated, supporting the ideas of national socialism, especially antisemitism. Another Parisian publisher and printer, G. Mazeyrie, was responsible for a satirical adaptation of the traditional *abécédaire* form, the *Abécédaire à l'usage des petits enfants qui apprennent à lire et des grandes personnes qui ne comprennent*

8. Rossignol, D., *Histoire de la propagande en France de 1940 à 1944*, PUF, 1991, p. 229.
9. Ibid.

Anon [N], Il était une fois (L'Histoire de Doulce France et Grojuif), Illustration by JB, NEF (1942): Grojuif impersonating Grandma.

pas encore le français.... In the case of Mazeyrie, the company's connections with the Germans are clearly documented;[10] the company was effectively requisitioned by the Nazis in October 1940, and from that date was a prolific source of propaganda attacking Masons, Jews, Bolsheviks and the British, all of whom appear as targets in the *abécédaire* referred to above. The *Bibliothèque de Documentation Internationale Contemporaine* (BDIC) also gives the Germans as the inspiration behind the other major fairy tale adaptation to have survived from this period, *L'Homme aux mains rouges* [The Man with Red Hands]. This beautifully illustrated tale is anonymous and undated, with no mention of publisher or printer, but does bear censorship inscriptions linking it with the German *Propaganda Abteilung*, the branch of Goebbels' Berlin-based propaganda machine that was hard at work in occupied Paris.

The guiding force behind the publication of these texts may have been German, but the literary traditions that they exploit are at the heart of French culture. Looking specifically at the use of the folk genre as a medium, one might argue that fairy tales or *Märchen* in one form or another are fundamental

10. Idem, p. 61.

to German literature also, not least through the efforts of the brothers Grimm. Delarue has demonstrated, however, that there are marked differences between the French tradition and other European folk tales, including those from Germany, which might be summarised as consisting of a greater degree of simplicity, fewer supernatural devices and a more human impulsion behind plot development in the French tradition.[11] Amidst the profusion of versions of the *Le Petit chaperon rouge* [Little Red Riding Hood] to have survived to the Second World War,[12] it is Perrault's version, that with which the overwhelming majority of French children would have been familiar, that has been chosen as the model (with only one slight but significant divergence), for the plot structure of *Doulce France et Grojuif. Barbe-Bleue* [Bluebeard], the model for *L'Homme aux mains rouges*, does not exist in the German tradition, the Grimm brothers having excluded it from their collection when they realised that the version they had intended to include had come to them direct from Perrault. The basic theme does exist in Germany in the form of the tale entitled *Fitchers Vogel* [Fitcher's Bird] published by the Grimm brothers, but the replacement of the human protagonist by a monstrous bird in that version, in addition to a number of other less drastic changes, distances it both from Perrault and *L'Homme aux mains rouges*.[13]

Why Choose a Fairy Tale?

The popularity and pervasiveness of the fairy tale in children's literature in France is one of the most compelling reasons for its choice as a propaganda medium, a reason compounded by a number of formal characteristics of the genre which render it particularly suitable to manipulation by the propagandist. Turning first to the enduring popularity of the genre, the favoured position of the fairy tale in the canon of children's literature received an unexpected boost between the two wars, when it provided publishers with the means of filling shortfalls in their output occasioned by the dearth of other suitable new material. Other popular authors such as the Comtesse de Ségur and Jules Verne also benefited from this situation, and the period saw many new editions and collections of these established favourites. Fairy tales were not just popular in their printed form, however. In a continuation of the oral tradition from which they originally sprang, public story-telling sessions were organised, as witnessed by the *Petit journal illustré* of 15 June 1924, which gave details of two girls who recounted fairy tales to groups of children gathered at their local bandstand,[14] and the activities of the librarians of the children's library the *Heure Joyeuse* in Paris.[15]

Tales of magic, both traditional and new, continued to be published during the Second World War,[16] but if such tales were very popular among children and among publishers, for whom they represented an assured source of income, they led to a certain degree of learned debate among some adults. The marvellous content of such tales came under severe scrutiny between the wars from educationalists such as Maria Montessori (who denounced them in a speech in London in 1921) and the American Sara Cone Bryant (who included them in her programme). Arnold Van Gennep defended their pedagogic value in the *Revue bleue* in 1921,[17] and Paul Hazard also defended them in 1927.[18] The controversy surrounding the genre focused above all on the fantastic element present in all such tales, and whether this

11. Delarue, P., *Le Conte populaire français*, Paris, 1957, vol 1, pp. 34-46.
12. See the works of Zipes, Soriano, and Delarue listed in the Bibliography.
13. Delarue (op. cit., p. 182) points out that Aarne-Thompson gives *Fitchers Vogel* a different classification number to *Barbe-Bleue*.
14.. Renonciat, op. cit., p. 66.
15. See Leriche, M., 'Les Contes dans l'éducation des enfants de 6 à 11 ans, ou l'Heure du Conte', in *La Revue du livre et des bibliothèques*, no. 12, 1934, pp. 261-272.
16. Details of these can be found in the *Bibliographie de la France* and in the catalogue of the *Heure Joyeuse*. Examples are: Huard, L.-L., *Quatre contes de fées*, Bordeaux, 1941; Platel, L., 'Le Sifflet magique' in *Contes pour les enfants* Paris 1942; Gisiger, H., *Tobio et ses aventures au pays des fées*, Neuchatel, 1941, and the sequel *Tobio détective au pays des fées*, 1942. The character of Barbe-Bleue was featured on the cover of the *Téméraire* of June 1st 1943.
17. Van Gennep, A., 'De la valeur pédagogique des contes de fées' in *Revue Bleue*, Paris, 1921, no. 19, pp. 602-606.
18. Hazard, P., 'Comment lisent les enfants' in *Revue des deux mondes* no. 42, 1927, pp 860-882.

was detrimental to a child's ability to distinguish between reality and fiction. Such a discussion clearly has interesting implications for the subsequent use of the genre as a medium for propaganda, and for the didactic efficacy of such texts in general.

The Didactic Qualities of Fairy Tales

According to Hazard, authors first tried to make fairy tales instructional in the 1920s (*'les fées deviendront institutrices'* [fairies were to become school-mistresses]),[19] but most experts are agreed in tracing a fundamental socialising imperative in the genre right back to Perrault. This imperative is made explicit in the morals appended to each tale in the original edition of Perrault's prose *contes*, although many subsequent editions omit them.[20] Even without the benefit of the moral, however, the tale of *Little Red Riding Hood*, to cite the example which interests us particularly here, is clearly cautionary, and this makes it an excellent vehicle for a 'moral' of a different nature. From a rather different perspective, one opponent of the Jewish publishing fraternity saw the fairy tale as a potential forerunner of the kind of moral poisoning that his enemies were apparently always on the look-out to promote; in 1923 the Abbé Bethléem railed against the Offenstadt press - '*Cette officine pornographique d'origine allemande*' [this den of pornography of German origin], accusing it of winning the fidelity of the nation's youth through the purveyance of fairy tales, only to corrupt its audience, once captured, with all kinds of brutal and depraving publications.[21]

Whatever the aims of such literature, Hazard is convinced that children are never duped by overtly didactic approaches, and that they are skilled in skipping over such passages, or in rejecting works in which the moral intention dominates.[22] Perhaps this is why the editors of some non-scholarly editions have chosen to omit the morals from the end of Perrault's prose tales. Henri Coston was of the same mind with regards to propaganda for children, suggesting that comic books should first of all amuse their young readers, the didactic purpose remaining skilfully disguised.[23] Whether or not the children themselves were duped, writers of propaganda prior to the Second World War had already seen the fairy tale as a genre worthy of their attentions. Perrault's ogre from *Le Petit Poucet* [Tom Thumb] had appeared in many political caricatures since Napoleonic times, usually as the embodiment of brutish authority,[24] and had gained a new lease of literary life in the First

19. Hazard , P., op. cit., p. 861.
20. The morals are referred to in the dedicatory letter to Elisabeth-Charlotte d'Orléans (Mademoiselle) *'Ils [les contes] renferment tous une Morale très sensée, et qui se découvre plus ou moins, selon le degré de pénétration de ceux qui les lisent'*. [They [the tales] all contain a very sensible Moral, which is more or less apparent, according to the degree of perception of those who read them]. This letter also refers to *'la louable impatience d'instruire les enfants'* [the laudable eagerness to instruct children] (Perrault, C., (ed M. Soriano) *Contes*, Garnier-Flammarion, 1991, pp. 245-246).
21. *'Elle s'empare des petits par l'attrait des images et des contes de fées; une fois grandis, elle les tient par des récits brutaux et dépravants, elle les mène ensuite, soit par des voies indirectes, soit par des voies ouvertes, à la polissonnerie et au libertinage'* [It captures the young through the attraction of pictures and fairy tales; when they have grown up, it holds them with violent and depraving stories, it then leads them, either by indirect means, or overtly, to licentiousness and debauchery] Abbé Bethléem, *Revue des lectures*, 15 mars 1923, quoted by Renonciat, op. cit., p. 28).
22. *'Pour sauter des paragraphes, des pages, des chapitres, quelle précoce habileté! Un coup d'oeil, un coup de pouce et cela suffit: ils ont senti venir le prêche et dextrement ils l'ont passé. C'est l'histoire qu'ils veulent retrouver; et si décidément on les abuse, tant pis pour le livre, il est condamné'* [What a precocious talent they have for skipping paragraphs, pages, chapters! A quick glance, a flick of the thumb and that's it; they sensed the sermon coming and skilfully avoided it. It is the story that they want to pick up again; and if one persists in taking advantage of them, too bad for the book, it is condemned] (Paul Hazard, op. cit., p. 863).
23. *'Le but de ces journaux pour enfants est de distraire, de satisfaire le goût et les aspirations des jeunes. Ce qu'il faut, ce n'est pas ennuyer et lasser cette clientèle enfantine, mais au contraire l'amuser tout en la guidant d'une main sûre et ferme vers les idéaux qui font la force des nations.* [The object of these comics is to amuse, to satisfy the tastes and the aspirations of the young. What is needed, is not to bore or to tire this juvenile audience, but on the contrary to amuse them, whilst all the while guiding them with a sure and firm hand towards the ideals that are the strength of a nation]. Coston, H., op. cit., p. 27.
24 . For a detailed discussion of the popular engravings associated with this tale, see Renonciat, A., *Petit Poucet dans la jonchée des feuilles*, Paris, Le Vieux Papier, 1990.

World War in '*L'Ogre et le Petit-Poucet*' by Emile Moselly [Emile Chenin] in *Contes de guerre pour Jean-Pierre*, (Berger-Levrault, 1918). In Moselly's tale, as with all of the propaganda produced in France in this period, the fairy tale style was used *against* the Germans (the Ogre), rather than in their favour.

Thanks to its very obvious nature as a cautionary tale, *Le Petit chaperon rouge* had also enjoyed a career in propaganda prior to the Second World War, in addition to the many unpoliticised versions that had flourished throughout Europe. In his investigation of *The Trials and Tribulations of Little Red Riding Hood*, Zipes charts many of these incarnations (though not *Doulce France et Grojuif*), picking up Hans-Wolf Jäger's suggestion that the story was given an anti-Jacobin context by both Tieck and Grimm.[25] Politics also have a role in the play *Red Riding Hood* by Thomason (1920) which cast Germany as the wolf and ended with the characters singing the *Marseillaise*. Finally, Zipes translates in full a version of the tale by the German writer Ulrich Link, which appeared in 1937, and which represents a biting satire of the German state and of Nazi propaganda.

Stylistic Elements in the Fairy Tale Facilitating Propaganda

To exploit a literary genre with which the reader is well-versed, enables a propagandist to lull his reader into accepting a new message under cover of a familiar wrapping. It may also inspire him to shock his reader into recognition of his message through a well-timed departure from the traditional script. Over and above the obvious advantages of adapting a genre with which readers are already familiar, however, the folk tale is composed of a number of structural and narrative elements that render it particularly suitable for exploitation by the propagandist. While these elements are best discussed in the context of specific works, a number of generalisations can be made. Simplicity is the fundamental key to the appeal of the genre, at structural, grammatical and lexical levels. Sub-plots are rarely encountered, sequences of events are, as Propp[26] has demonstrated, limited, predictable, and often used in repeat or symmetrical arrangements (cf the arrival of the Wolf and Red Riding Hood at Grandma's cottage). Resulting in part from the oral origins of such tales, the linguistic simplicity is further enhanced by a number of repeated verbal formulae that give the text rhythm and dramatic effect, and help to anchor the tale in the reader's, or listener's, memory while imparting a certain sense of involvement in the narrative process, and perhaps, by extension, in the story itself. Again *Little Red Riding Hood* provides a good illustration of this technique, in the question and answer session at the end of the tale, where not only are the queries and responses formulaic, but where the final response of the wolf is often addressed directly to the audience by an adult reader.[27] Characterisation is marked by a strong element of stereotype and exaggeration (the richest, the poorest, the most beautiful...), which, added to the stock functions of certain characters (the stepmother, the witch, the wolf), aids in the rapid identification of 'goodies' and 'baddies'.

If the genre is notable for its simplicity on a structural/linguistic level, there are many more complicated processes occurring under the surface. For the original author and for the propagandist alike, the restricted length of the fairy tale is conducive to sustained allegory; moral or social in the case of the former, political in the case of the latter. The fantastic devices natural

25. Zipes, J., *The Trials and Tribulations of Little Red Riding Hood*, Heinemann, London, 1983. pp. 17 and 18.
26. Propp, V., *Morphology of the Folktale*, Indiana University, 1968.
27. This was clearly the original intention of Perrault who worked from oral accounts of the tale, and who noted at this juncture in the text of 1695: '*On prononce ces mots d'une voix forte pour faire peur à l'enfant comme si le loup l'allait manger*' [One pronounces these words in a loud voice to frighten the child as if the wolf were about to eat them] (Soriano, M., *Les Contes de Perrault, culture savante et traditions populaires* , Gallimard, 1977, p. 80).

to the genre and the strong element of exaggeration are also invaluable in this domain as they allow a more serious message to be portrayed in a highly entertaining and striking manner. In addition to the cautionary or moral aspect built into Perrault's tales, however, there are other levels of 'hidden' or privileged reading, to be absorbed at a subconscious level or enjoyed consciously by those with greater perception, as Perrault himself pointed out in the dedicatory letter that accompanied the first edition of the tales. Rouger gives examples of slightly risqué asides incorporated into the seemingly innocent texts of *La Belle au bois dormant* [Sleeping Beauty] and *Le Petit Poucet*,[28] and the fact that these are considered 'above the heads' or unsuitable for children by some editors is confirmed by the exclusion of the example from *Le Petit Poucet* in at least one non-scholarly edition of the tale.[29] The timelessness of the tales, introduced by those immortal words '*Il était une fois*' or 'Once upon a time' also enables the adept author to introduce a set of essentially anachronistic references to the present day into his narrative, thus enhancing the relevance of the moral/political message to the contemporary reader. Perrault himself indulged in a number of such references in his tales, incorporating details of the personality of Louis XIV, a 17th-century royal wedding, and of the palace at Versailles.[30]

For the writer of agitation propaganda, the violence inherent in many of the tales is particularly valuable, for, coupled with the elements of exaggeration and fantasy, it enables wicked characters to behave in a manner which is truly evil (one only needs to re-read *Le Petit Poucet* to be convinced of this exceptionally violent streak in Perrault's tales). The internal realism of the fairy tale[31] renders this trait particularly dangerous when it is a question of manipulating the young reader. The conventions of the genre render such evil actions believable within the context of the tale, they even make them inescapable as a natural extension of the character's psychological and physical makeup. Give the wicked character an identity from the real world, that of a Jew for example, and a child may well believe the Jew capable of such evil deeds in real life.

Even more disturbing, perhaps, when the fairy tale is used for propaganda purposes, is the fact that the comparative absence of a great deal of overt magic in the French tradition highlights the fact that actions and effects are created by human impulsion. The ultimate message in Perrault is that '*la source de la magie est dans l'âme humaine*' [the source of the magic is in the human soul][32] that is, that despite all their fantasy trappings and their literary presentation, these are *true* stories in terms of psychological realism. This is particularly well demonstrated in the tale *Riquet à la houppe*, less familiar in English collections, in which an ugly prince and a stupid princess become attractive and intelligent in the eyes of the other, ostensibly through the intervention of a magic spell, but in fact as a result of their love for each other. This psychological dimension, while adding value to the fairy tale when it exists in its pure form, becomes a dangerous weapon in the hands of the propagandist.

The Case of '*Le Petit chaperon rouge*'

This tale is acknowledged as holding a unique position in Perrault's works as the most overtly cautionary of all the prose *contes*. In its oral origins it was

28. Perrault, C., (ed G. Rouger), *Contes de Perrault*, Paris, Garnier, 1967, p. xlvii.
29. I have not investigated this omission in other editions, but it is certainly absent from the Flammarion edition of *Les Contes de Perrault* illustrated by Pierre Noury, published in the 1920s.
30. Rouger, op. cit., pp. xlii and xliii.
31. See Hazard, who discusses in some detail '*ce réel que l'inexplicable interrompt sans l'abolir*' [this reality that the inexplicable interrupts without destroying] (Hazard, P., op. cit., p. 869).
32. Montégut, E., *Des fées et de leur littérature en France*, quoted by Rouger, op. cit., p. xlv.

probably a genuine warning against straying into lonely areas where wolves continued to roam freely, as they did in much of Europe in the Middle Ages, and was thus a fictionalised, but not fantastic, portrayal of reality. Even the anthropomorphic qualities of the wolf were not originally based in the realms of fantasy, as people at this time genuinely believed in the existence of werewolves, the number of werewolf trials in the 15th–17th centuries testifying to the seriousness of this belief. Historians of the genre are united in agreeing that it was Perrault himself who first adapted the tale to endow it with a symbolic meaning that comprised the socialising aim of warning young maidens of the dangers of straying from the path of duty, and of fraternising with strangers, particularly male 'wolves'. The sexual element of the moral is made particularly clear in the moral affixed to the end of the tale.

Successive generations of writers have added many refinements to the actual tale, and projected a number of surprising interpretations onto even the earliest versions. The best known modification of the tale is that of the Grimm brothers (*Rotkäppchen*, 1812), which gave a dramatically new twist to the ending of the tale by introducing a valorous woodcutter to cut open the wolf's stomach, extract Red Riding Hood and Grandma, and to aid them in weighing down the wolf's stomach with stones, leading to his sudden death. According to the theoretical leanings of subsequent critics, this ending either conforms to reality by representing the most likely means of our heroine being saved when in the depths of the forest (assuming one accepts the feasibility of escaping lupine ingestion unharmed), or is equally realistic as a demonstration of the phallocratic dominance of a male-orientated society over the frivolous and ineffectual weaker sex[33]. You pays your money...[34] What the Grimms' ending does appear to do, is to dilute the danger by which Red Riding Hood, and by extension the reader, is threatened, by suggesting that some outside agency will ultimately come to the rescue - a very profound and significant modification of Perrault's original message.

Study of Two Propaganda Texts

'Doulce France et Grojuif'

The title of the tale '*Doulce France et Grojuif*' is sufficient to suggest the nature of the pastiche that is to follow. This version of the well-known story presents Doulce France [Sweet France] in the heroine's role, Grojuif [Fatjew] as the Wolf, with Mother and Grandma playing themselves, although the latter is given the added burden of appearing under the highly symbolic name of '*Vérité*' or 'Truth'. Close analysis demonstrates that this version is an exceptionally faithful reproduction of the original Perrault version (see Appendix 2), with only a few marked divergences, most notably in the ending of the tale. Here a switch is made from Perrault to Grimm, with Doulce France being rescued from Grojuif's clutches not by a woodcutter, but by '*un des fils de la nouvelle France*' - a *Légionnaire* according to the uniform he wears in the illustration. The text is illustrated by nine scenes from the tale, which again serve to establish a close connection between this story and the traditional tale (see illustration, p.26). All the settings and characters would be suitable illustrations for the Perrault version, with the exception of the final picture, featuring France's saviour, and for the character of Grojuif

33. Fromm even disagrees with this interpretation, qualifying the huntsman as 'the conventional father figure without real weight' and defining the tale as 'a story of triumph by man-hating woman' (Fromm, E., op. cit., p. 241).
34. One of the most detailed psychoanalyses of this tale is to be found in Bettelheim, B., *The Uses of Enchantment. The Meaning and Importance of Fairy Tales*, Penguin, 1976, pp. 166–183.

himself. When Grojuif first appears, his silhouette is essentially lupine in nature, but this resolves itself into a much more hybrid monster in successive scenes. Interestingly, the illustrator has avoided too 'human' an appearance for the anti-hero, unlike many illustrators of the classic tale, and has gone rather for a horrible fantasy figure with a disproportionately large hooked nose.

Turning first to the similarities between the two texts, these can perhaps best be appreciated by comparing the two stories, reproduced in parallel in Appendix 2. A comparative study reveals first of all that the texts are almost identical in length — approximately 650 words (excluding the moral in verse appended to the Perrault version). The propaganda text follows every plot development of the original, but is expressed in a simpler and slightly more concise form (see below), thus allowing the inclusion of France's rescue at the end of the story without exceeding the number of words in the original. The lexical similarity between the two texts is marked. As a rough guide, approximately 40 per cent of the original words used by Perrault are reproduced in an identical form and in a substantially identical context in the propaganda version, and while the later version has modernised Perrault's grammar and vocabulary to a certain extent in a quest for greater clarity, it has retained the notable archaisms already present in the original, thus establishing a clear link with the pre-text and retaining much of the flavour of it. The archaic verb '*seyer*' is retained early in the propaganda text to confirm the literary *bona fides* of this version already established with the classic opening '*Il était une fois*'. Both of these devices also serve, as they do in Perrault, to perpetuate the 'timeless' convention of the genre. The second notable archaism, the use of the verb '*choir*' in the instructions that the Grandmother and subsequently the Wolf/Grojuif issue ('*tire la chevillette, la bobinette cherra*') was perhaps originally included to suggest the age and peasant background of the grandmother. It remains one of the most memorable phrases in the text, having, as Soriano suggests, some of the qualities of a popular tongue-twister.[35] Again its retention by the propagandist demonstrates a desire to highlight the links between the two texts and to profit from the most popular features of the original. Even more striking than the similarities in structure and language is the way in which the antisemitic message of the propaganda text is so well adapted to the story-line of the original. Because of the simplicity of the tale and the clearly defined but two-dimensional characters, one set of players can easily be replaced by another; the story, even the vocabulary, remain the same, but the ultimate message is far more sinister.

The propagandist has not been able to resist some additional touches of his own, however, to make his message even clearer, and to introduce a comic effect in the characterisation of Grojuif while reinforcing all the prejudices connected with the stereotypical portrait of the Jew. Thus, in a departure from the original, Grojuif reverts to his own voice ('*sa voix naturelle*') for the question and answer session with Doulce France, enabling the author to make much of his Jewish accent. A supplementary question is added to the famous list of enquiries to highlight not only the supposedly typical Jewish nose, but also the cupiditous nature it is meant to denote ('*Ma*

35. Soriano, M., op. cit., pp. 153-154.

mère'grand, que vous avez un grand nez! - C'est bour mieux renifler les bedides affaires ma ville' [Grandma, what a big nose you have! – All de bedder to zniv out little business deals by dear]). The supposedly insinuating nature of the Jew is also introduced in the propaganda text when Grojuif first meets France ('*[il] se fit gentil*'), and the grasping hooked fingers which featured in so many posters of the period are not omitted; the '*fils de la nouvelle France*' [the son of the new France] arrives just in time to deliver France from their grasp ('*pour délivrer Doulce France des doigts crochus de Grojuif*').

All these stereotypical attributes are notable additions to the text, but the most blatant antisemitic attack comes in a deformation of the existing text. In Perrault's version, the Wolf kills and eats Grandma because he hasn't eaten for more than three days. In the antisemitic propaganda, he does so to satisfy his bloodthirsty tendencies, and it is noted that he habitually kills and eats the flesh for pleasure (as indicated by the imperfect tense of '*tuait*' and '*dévorait*'). The impact of this accusation is made all the more sinister by the causal relationship expressed in each text which relates to the whole question of the inherent realism and 'human' impulsion in Perrault's fairy tales. If we accept that it is realistic, even normal, that a wolf should kill through intense hunger, we are more likely to accept, even subconsciously, the logic given to explain Grojuif's actions.

It is all the more surprising in view of this vicious attack, that the author of the propaganda version has not taken the opportunity to exploit one feature of the original tale that was particularly suited to antisemitic propaganda of this period. A marked element in such literature in both France and Germany is the concentration on the lecherous nature of the Jew, and his compelling desire to corrupt the virtuous and pure French/German maidens. In Germany this theme featured in a picture book of 1936 published by Streicher (Nuremberg) entitled *Trau keinem Fuchs auf grüner Heid, Und keinem Jud bei seinem Eid!* (Never trust a fox on a green heath, And never trust a Jew on his oath!)[36]. In France this theme was taken up by Henri Coston in his attack on Offenstadt (see above). If the Germans concentrated above all on the threat that the Jews represented to the purity of the race, the French highlighted the sexual and moral aspects of the threat, and thus it is all the more interesting that nothing

36. *Was ist der Jud ein armer Wicht!*	The Jew is a poor wretch!
Mag seine eignen Frauen nicht!	His own women don't appeal to him!
Er meint, er sei entsetzlich schlau,	He thinks he's teribly clever
Wenn er sich stiehlt 'ne deutsche Frau.	When he steals a German woman.
[...]	[...]
Der Vater zu der Tochter sagt:	The father says to his daughter:
"In mir ein schrecklich Sorgen nagt!	'A dreadful worry plagues me!
Wir sind doch reinen Bluts!	We are all of pure blood!
Du aber gehst aus Eigennutz	You, however, out of self-interest,
Um schöne Kleider und um Geld	For the sake of fine clothes and money
Zum Juden Sali Rosenfeld	Are seeing the Jew Sali Rosenfeld
Und meinst, du wirst gar seine Frau!	And even talk about becoming his wife!
Das geht nicht, wird nicht, hör' genau:	It's not on, no way, now listen well:
Ans Wagenjoch der guten Kuh	One would never hitch a dachshund
Spannt niemals man den Dackel zu!	In a yoke intended for a fine cow!
Das ist ja die Unmöglichkeit!	It's just not possible!
[...]	

(Bauer, E., *Trau keinem Fuchs auf grüner Heid, Und keinem Jud bei seinem Eid!* Stürmer-Verlag, Nuremberg, 1936).

was made of the 'nakedness' of Perrault's wolf, and his invitation to Red Riding Hood to join him in bed. In Perrault, the young girl not only accepts the invitation, but undresses without prompting, and the author himself makes the rather risqué comment that she is surprised at the appearance of the wolf '*en son déshabillé*'. The sexual element is evident in Perrault even without this aside or the reinforcement provided by the moral at the end of the tale, and one can only speculate as to why the propagandist chose to ignore it. Ignore it he certainly does, for Doulce France is only invited to approach the bed ('*viens près de mon lit*'), not to enter it, and France is surprised only by his '*allure étrange*' [strange appearance], as Grojuif is in fact not naked having dressed himself in the clothes of the Grandma. This last factor is part of the apparent explanation as to why the propagandist chose to abandon an ideal opportunity more or less handed to him on a plate and links up with the final major departure from the original text.

In giving Grandma the highly symbolic name of '*Vérité*' [Truth], the author of the propaganda text has added an allegorical dimension to the tale that is entirely absent from the original. This addition, introduced in the second sentence of the story appears to suggest an underlying discussion of fundamental moral abstracts, but in reality only seems to have been included to enable a further dig at the Jewish stereotype, whose inherent hypocrisy is demonstrated by his 'putting on the clothes of Truth' once he has killed and eaten Grandma. In deviating from the original model, the shortcomings of the propaganda author become apparent. Having given Grandma an apparently symbolic function, an acceptable move given the symbolic importance of Doulce France (not just an individual French girl, but the whole nation at risk from Judaïsm), the allegory is not pursued. The grandmother neither says nor does anything that particularly links her to the virtue she is deemed to represent. In line with the original version, we are told that the grandmother adores her young grand-daughter, whereas it would perhaps have been more significant in symbolic terms if *Doulce France* were to adore *la Vérité*. There is no obvious significance to Truth giving France a red cap, especially as the cap is given no explicit symbolism, and while the fact that Truth is ailing could be a reference to contemporary events, the allusion is not pursued. No indication is given as to how the biscuits and butter the child brings her grandmother might help Truth's indisposition, as these objects are not endowed with any alternative qualities. While the ending of the tale is perfectly consistent with the political message of the propaganda story, it confirms the lack of cohesion at a more complex level of allegory. The woodcutter is '*un fils de la nouvelle France*', but apparently no relation to '*la Doulce France*', who is also distinct from the France whose skies are now filled with the 'warm rays of Truth'. As this last reference suggests, it is the sun which finally takes on the allegorical attributes of Truth, and Grandma, allegorical significance and all, appears to have been abandoned in the belly of Grojuif.

Setting aside this unsuccessful attempt to embellish the original story, and the other additions referred to above, the propaganda version of *Le Petit chaperon rouge* demonstrates very effectively the techniques of grammatical and narrative simplification that can be employed to make an uncomplicated text even clearer in order to ensure the successful transmission of a political message. The most consistent technique employed by the propagandist here is to split Perrault's sentences, already very straightforward grammatically-speaking, into their major components, creating new, shorter, unsubordinated sentences.[37] Thus the 35 sentences in Perrault's version become 51 in the later text, only five of these being accounted for by completely new material (the reference to Grojuif's nose, and the ending). Average sentence length falls in the later version from 19 words to 12, and although the shortest 'sentence' in both stories is the two-word 'Toc, toc', the longest in the propaganda text is 29 (*Grojuif la voyant lui dit* ...) compared with Perrault's 50 (*Le Loup se mit à courir* ...). The most common means of splitting a sentence is by replacing conjunctions such as 'et' and 'car' by a full stop and commencing a new sentence, or by taking out the relative pronoun 'qui' and beginning a new sentence with the relevant personal pronoun. Perrault's use of the semi-colon as a linking technique is also discontinued in the propaganda text, again being replaced by the start of a new sentence. To streamline the narrative, a number of phrases not essential to the plot are stripped from the original, resulting in a somewhat starker exposition of the events and detracting from the consummate elegance of the original. Thus Perrault's phrase '*Le petit chaperon rouge tira la chevillette, et la porte s'ouvrit*' [Little Red Riding Hood pulled the latch, and the door opened] is replaced by the abrupt '*Doulce France entra*' [Doulce France entered]. This represents an economy of effort on both the author's and reader/listener's part, but an impoverishment of a text that has so carefully set up a series of references to the '*chevillette*' as part of a richly textured aural experience.[38]

L'Homme aux mains rouges

Simplification is also evident in this propaganda version of the *Bluebeard* story, resulting in a reduction of the overall length of the later text to approximately two thirds that of the original. In this tale, there is far less direct use of the original language of the Perrault version, although there is sufficient to suggest that the author had access to the original at the time of writing his or her adaptation. Significantly the highest proportion of direct transcription appears on the first page of the propaganda version (approximately 37 per cent of the page) perhaps to attract the reader's attention by its similarity to Perrault and firmly to establish the connection between the two texts.[39] In the remaining 6 pages (as originally laid out in the published book), 1 has approximately 2 per cent of 'original Perrault' text, 2 have less than 1 per cent and the others have none. Sentences are much longer than those of *Doulce France et Grojuif*, the 1018 words being divided into only 25 sentences. With an average length of 41 words, the shortest sentence has 12 words (the concluding sentence), but the longest is a massive 97, exclamation marks, with which the text is liberally spattered, rarely signifying the end of a sentence.

Linguistically, this then is a much looser pastiche of Perrault than *Doulce France et Grojuif*, and as a result it loses some of the dramatic effect and lyrical appeal of the original. This is particularly noticeable with regard to the use of archaisms and repetition of verbal formulae, as discussed above. In the

37. Lüthi informs us that Wilhelm Grimm carried out a similar process when he adapted popular folk tales for the Fairy Tales, being particularly careful to eliminate subordinate clauses (Lüthi, M., *Once Upon a Time. On the Nature of Fairy Tales*, Indiana University Press, 1976, p. 37).
38. Other stylistic comparisons can be made from a study of the parallel texts in Appendix 2.
39. It is somewhat surprising, therefore, that this version begins with the less frequently used introduction '*Il y avait une fois*' (my emphasis), which is not used in *Barbe-Bleue*, which begins with the more familiar '*Il était une fois*'.

final scene of the tale, the author of *L'Homme aux mains rouges* has eliminated the twice-repeated reference to '*le soleil qui poudroie, et l'herbe qui verdoie*' (not even replacing it with a more modern version) and greatly diminishes the dramatic suspense of the original tale, by reducing the number of times the heroine looks for salvation (from four times to only twice). The modern author also cuts the character of the sister who features in the original and with whom the heroine engages in a series of formulaic questions and answers while waiting to be saved.

In general terms, descriptive detail and literary embellishment in *L'Homme aux mains rouges* have been stripped down to the minimum necessary to retain a strong association with the original story, without necessarily reproducing all of the literary effects created in the original. What descriptive elements have been retained, are adapted to suit the new meaning of the tale and the characters who feature in it. Thus this story centres on the actions of a powerful ruler, the eponymous 'hero' of the tale, who wishes to marry the beautiful princess Europa. He leaves her in the Kremlin, in charge of his possessions, while he travels to Siberia in the far flung reaches of his domain, pausing only to warn her on pain of death against entering his castle in Katyn. True to the impulsions of her 17th century alter ego, the princess cannot resist the temptation to do that which has been forbidden, and on entering a locked room in the forbidden castle, discovers the bodies of the ruler's previous brides, Princess Poland, Grand Duchess Lithuania etc. As in Perrault, the key falls to the ground and is covered with a blood stain that cannot be removed, which alerts the ruler to her discovery on his return. The bloody-handed despot swears by the damned soul of Lenin to revenge himself of Europa, and she retreats to the highest tower of the castle to call her people to her aid. Despite the divergence from the Perrault version at this dramatic climax, the outcome in the propaganda text is ultimately the same, for the Princess is saved by the timely arrival of the noble Prince Germain, who destroys the despot and liberates the Princess. In recognition of this valorous deed she places herself under his protection 'thus assuring years of Peace and Prosperity for many long years for the entire world' (see Appendix 3 for a transcription of this tale in its entirety).

Even before the despot is revealed as Stalin by Prince Germain on the penultimate page of the text, many clues have been laid down as to his true identity. Elements from the original fairy tale are cleverly adapted to give the opportunity for descriptions of the abundant cereal harvest and rich mineral resources of the despot's dominions, and to provide the names of his previous mistresses, Francia and Espana, '*dames de la cour*', a reference to the factions that 'flirted' with Stalin during the French Popular Front and the Spanish Civil war. John Bull is also named as an ally of *L'Homme aux mains rouges*. The reference to the bodies discovered in Katyn is not only the direct inspiration behind the text, but it also helps to date this publication, which was presumably written soon after the discovery of the murdered Polish officers in the Forest of Katyn in early 1943. Stalin himself had started to feature as a villain in French propaganda from December 1940 with the beginning of Hitler's drive towards the East entitled 'operation Barbarossa' - a name to conjure with in this context!

In addition to the transparent references to Stalinist Russia in the written text, the illustrations of this tale are loaded with symbolic allusions to the Red Peril, and also bring out the racial stereotypes associated with the Bolshevik, characteristics not explicitly referred to in the text itself. Stalin and his henchmen have the thick eyebrows, slanted eyes, and hooked nose typical of visual representation of the Soviets in this period, and Stalin is further typified by his characteristic thick drooping moustache. Europa and Germain, on the other hand, are clearly Aryan. Stalin is surrounded by many symbols of his nationality; a tame (Russian) bear dances at court in the first picture, in the second a bear skin covers the sledge in which Stalin and Europa ride. Red stars feature in profusion, as do the hammer and sickle which are cunningly inserted into every illustration, as part of a flag standard, as a candle stick, as wall paper, etc. The troops of the noble Prince Germain in keeping with the 'timeless' flavour of the fairy tale, are dressed in suits of armour, but the helmets they wear are identical to those worn by the German troops in the 1940s (see illustration below).

Anon, L'Homme aux mains rouges, n.d.: The marriage of Princess Europa and Prince Germain.

As in *Doulce France et Grojuif*, the propagandist author of *L'Homme aux mains rouges* has not included any reference to the morals, for there were two, appended to the 1697 Perrault version of *Barbe-Bleue*. One of the reasons for this could have been that they were simply not aware of their existence, many modern editors having chosen not to include any of the '*moralités*' appended to the original tales in their editions. For those familiar with these morals, it is immediately clear, however, why their omission would perhaps have been a foregone conclusion in the propaganda version of the *Bluebeard* story. The first moral stresses the curiosity of the woman, and concentrates on the deceptions encountered as a result of attempting to satisfy this particular vice. While the propaganda text, interestingly, does comment on the weakness of Europa in wishing to satisfy her curiosity in Katyn,[40] too great a reflection on the participation of Europa in her brush with Stalinism might deflect attention from the true villain of the piece, *l'Homme aux mains rouges*, alias Joseph Stalin. The second moral essentially reduces the dramatic story to an allegory for domestic squabbles and the battle of the sexes - of no interest, and again a potential diversion, in the eyes of the propaganda writer.

The violent nature of these propaganda stories may shock, but the violence they contain is all to be found in their 17th century models. Even the cannibalistic instincts attributed to the Jew have their equivalent in the Ogres and Ogresses of Perrault's originals, in tales such as *Tom Thumb* and in the latter part of *Sleeping Beauty* (sometimes excluded from modern editions). What is particularly shocking, perhaps, is the fact that rather than embodying abstract human characteristics, such as greed, lust, envy etc., exaggerated for greater effect, these propaganda stories pin this antisocial behaviour on real sections of the community, and by identifying fictional characters with living individuals, transform their actions from the allegorical into the representational.

If the story lines, characterisation and narrative structures of the classic fairy tale are well-suited to aggressive agitation propaganda, however, this was not their only value to the propagandists of Vichy France. To convey the importance of *Travail, Famille and Patrie* to the younger members of society, and to encourage them to assist in the renaissance of their country, elements of the fairy tale genre were combined with other aspects of traditional children's literature, to create a softer image with which to woo the young reader. These are the Golden Age and Utopian idylls discussed in the next section.

40. '*La curiosité est un vilain défaut et malgré toutes ses qualités, la Princesse EUROPA était une petite curieuse [...]*' [Curiosity killed the cat, and despite all her good qualities, EUROPA was an inquisitive little thing] (op. cit., p. 6).

III
France the Fairy-tale Kingdom

Models from the Third Republic

When the propagandists ofVichy France sought a suitable literary genre through which to instil the tenets of the *Révolution nationale* into the younger generation, it was in the school reading books of the Third Republic that they found an important source of inspiration. Setting aside those volumes composed exclusively of extracts from the French classics, carefully selected for their relevance to the moral position prescribed by the Republic, the late nineteenth and early twentieth centuries saw the publication of a number of educational story books specially written to encapsulate and expound the importance of patriotism, family life and the work ethic. The format and narrative style of these books provided a useful example of how a strong didactic imperative could be made more palatable by the introduction of an elementary story-line; and because the message these books were conveying was so similar to that of the *Etat français*, some elements of these narratives could be integrated with little modification into the later propaganda texts (see below).

The existence of a strong moralising trend in nineteenth-century school literature served another important function, in that it consolidatedVichy's claim that they were reviving the kind of moral standards that had ensured the country's greatness in former times, before the likes of jazz, falling birthrates and the Popular Front had led to widespread degeneracy and, almost inevitably, to the fall of France in 1940. The benefits of such a stance were two-fold. Firstly, the régime was able to create a glowing image of a former Golden Age, which all elements of society should strive to recapture. Secondly, the pre-war lapse in standards conveniently exculpatedVichy from any part in the crushing military defeat so recently experienced. In the official view of events, the increasing degeneracy of the nation had so sapped its vital energy and resolve that its future was in some doubt even before the intervention of external forces and despite the heroic way in which the country and its new leader rallied in the final hours. This explanation had the happy consequence of exonerating the Nation, and more specifically the *Etat français*, from any charges of military or diplomatic incompetence associated with the *débâcle*, and of glossing over any blame to be apportioned in the matter to the Germans, with whom the government had now openly embarked on a policy of collaboration. Furthermore, it hammered a further nail into the coffin of the Popular Front, whose actions were to be held up to public scrutiny in the trials at Riom (February - April 1942).

The school reading books with which the propaganda texts reviewed in this section have most in common, are publications such as *Le Tour de la*

France par deux enfants (*cours moyen*) (Paris, Belin, 1877) and *Jeannot et Jeannette* (Paris, Hachette, 1924). These stories, and a number of others like them, centre on the experiences of two or more children who embark on a voyage of discovery both physical and metaphorical, during which they uncover not only the physical attributes of their native land and the achievements of its people, but also the moral values that have served to make France great. The use of a journey as a means of introducing a wide variety of characters and settings is, of course, a standard literary technique, as is the symbolic significance of the device. In line with the educational imperative of such stories, the settings are essentially realistic, enabling a very factual description of France's many riches, but an element of propaganda is already present, as Emmelina points out, with some aspects of contemporary life often being enhanced to produce a more glowing portrait of society.[1]

The choice of children as the main protagonists in such stories is clearly essential. Firstly, it provides an important source of identification and emulation for the young readers, who will more readily share in the exploits and emotions of children of their own age. Secondly, it allows for a highly simplified and didactic approach to the introduction of factual material, as a succession of helpful adults encountered in the course of the journey take it upon themselves to explain the latest agricultural and industrial inventions to the children. Further opportunities for didacticism are often built into such stories by the convention of making one child much younger than the other. More factual information is thus imparted to the reader as the elder child gives his younger sibling the benefit of his superior learning, and the child-like style of these impromptu lessons is further designed to make them more accessible to the young reader. In *Le Tour de la France* this capacity to instruct is extended even further when the younger child is given a book about the great men of French history, from which he periodically reads aloud during the course of their journey.

In all of these improving stories, as in much of the very similar English fiction for children of the same period, the protagonists are either orphans (such is the case in *Le Tour de la France*), or in some way separated from their parents. In nineteenth century English fiction, this convention allows the bourgeois ideals of equal opportunity for all and the importance of individual effort, to be played out in a most effective manner.[2] In *Le Tour de la France*, although strengthened in mind and body by their improving odyssey around France, the young orphans long for a stable family life, a dream which is eventually fulfilled. For the *Etat français*, the advantages of employing such a device are manifest. While family life can still be held up as an ideal, the experiences of the individual and their contribution to society can also be brought into relief. Emphasis on individual effort, as Ozouf points out, also provided a constant reminder of the achievements of Philippe Pétain, who through his application and devotion to duty, rose from the relative obscurity of an agricultural background to the eminent position of leader of the *Etat français*.[3]

The rural origins of the *Maréchal* and his unshakeable belief in the importance of France's agricultural tradition (summed up in his famous pronouncement '*la terre, elle, ne ment pas*') also find expression in Vichy

1. Emmelina, J., 'La "littérature" de l'école primaire. L'idéologie des livres de lecture courante dans l'Enseignement primaire, en France, depuis la IIIe République', in *Idéologie et propagande en France*, Paris, Picard, 1987, p. 182.
2. Kramnick, op. cit., p. 217.
3. Ozouf, J. and M., 'Le Thème du patriotisme dans les manuels primaires' in *Mouvement social*, Paris, no. 49, 1964, p. 14.

propaganda for children, exploiting similar trends already apparent in pre-war literature. As in England, the industrial revolution in France found its way into didactic literature for children, with texts such as *Le Tour de la France* praising the technical advances of the day. Emmelina characterises such stories as belonging to the '*esprit épique*', exalting the harmony that existed between their readers and the developing world around them. As industry advanced, however, and people began to find themselves the slaves rather than the masters of the machines they had invented, '*l'esprit romanesque*', a nostalgia for the rural lifestyle of the past, began to appear in children's literature as it did in many other branches of the media at this time. Geography books contributed to this trend, with increasingly idyllic presentations of the natural attractions of France.

In the war, an explicitly moral dimension was added to this trend with the equation: country = good, town = corruption, and a corresponding rejection of all that was associated with urban life, ranging from egotism and loose living to falling birthrates and jazz.[4] Politically, the recapture of this quasi-mythical Golden Age of a rural, agricultural France, peopled by honest, hard-working farmers and artisans, became the avowed goal of the *Révolution nationale* and the promotion of the myth in turn legitimised the régime which promised to help the people achieve it.[5]

As the idyllic nature of France was raised to ever-increasing preeminence, so the language used to portray the nation moved inexorably into the realms of allegory. Already in *Le Tour de la France*, what Emmelina describes as a quasi-mystical and allegorical language was used to portray France, and although his claim that France is presented as a kind of divine being is somewhat exaggerated,[6] it is perhaps not surprising that the language and imagery of religion should feature in the portrayal of these secular visions of the Garden of Eden and the Fall.[7] Religious language and imagery is used in all of the Second World War texts reviewed in this section, particularly in the evocation of the disaster that smites the nation (see below, *Il était une fois un pays heureux* and *Six petits enfants et treize étoiles*) and in the portrayal of Pétain, in both text and illustrations, who takes on many God/Christ/Saint-like characteristics.

What is particularly striking about the texts analysed in this section, especially when they are seen as part of a more widespread tendency encompassing the publications studied in Sections II and IV, is their use of elements of the fairy tale, a genre not obviously exploited by their school-book predecessors. In *Le Tour de la France*, the magical acts portrayed in fairy tales are used as a standard of comparison in the description of the mechanical wonders of the industrial revolution — to the greater glory of French ingenuity and greatly to the detriment of fairy stories which are implicitly dismissed as arrant nonsense compared to the realities of modern France.[8] Similarly, the captain of a ship on which the two orphans travel, mistakenly assumes that the younger boy is reading fairy tales, when in fact he is reading the improving book about the great men of France referred to above. The implied comparison between the two types of literature is again highly unfavourable to the fairy tale.[9]

In the propaganda texts discussed below, the elements borrowed from the fairy tale tradition are not used as they are in the stories considered in

4. For a detailed study of the importance Vichy gave to folklore, regionalism etc, see Faure, C., *Le Projet culturel de Vichy*, Presses universitaires de Lyon, 1989.
5. Girardet describes this transformation - a standard operation in times of national crisis - in the following terms: '*C'est par rapport à l'image, idéologiquement reconstruite, d'une nation disparue de l'histoire, mais dont on entend retrouver la mémoire, exalter la grandeur passée, que se trouve légitimé le combat à entreprendre pour en assurer la résurrection*' (Girardet, R., op. cit., p. 104).
6. Emmelina, op. cit., p. 177.
7. Idem, p. 176.
8. Op. cit., pp. 48-9, 115.
9. Idem, p. 202.

the previous section, as a sinister or cunning parody, but in the spirit in which they were originally employed, for the purposes of enchantment, for the creation of a fairy-tale kingdom. The difference between these narratives and more traditional fairy stories is that in the latter the children know that the magic kingdom does not really exist, whereas here they are being very actively encouraged to believe that it really does, and that they are living in it.

Case Studies

Origins

Of the three propaganda stories discussed here, only one was officially associated with the government office, the *Bureau de Documentation du Chef d'Etat. Il était une fois un pays heureux* by Victor Dancette was published by the Editions de la Générale Publicité in Paris for the *Bureau* in March 1943, and as the final page proudly declares, 50 luxury numbered editions of the story were printed for Pétain himself. Ironically, Dancette is also the author of a strongly *anti*-Vichy text, also published by Générale Publicité, which appeared in two parts soon after the Liberation, entitled *La Bête est morte. La guerre mondiale chez les animaux*[10]. The latter work makes no mention of the earlier publication or ostensible affiliations of the author or indeed of the publisher, and somewhat paradoxically, neither of the two books can be faulted in its obvious conviction, not to say missionary zeal....

Although the other texts, *Six petits enfants et treize étoiles* and *Bonjour la France!* were not published by government agencies, peritextual and biographical details confirm close links with the régime. The author of *Six petits enfants*, Paluel-Marmont, was a prolific author of children's books, including a number concerning Pétain, about whom he lectured in Parisian lycées. A 'biography' of Pétain, written by Paluel-Marmont and discussed in the next section, was published for the charity initiative organised in the *Maréchal*'s name by the Secours National in 1941 - the 'Secours National Entr'aide d'hiver du Maréchal'. *Six petits enfants*, was published in 1942 by the Parisian firm Editions et Publications Françaises, and was illustrated by Lucien Boucher.

'Jaboune', alias Jean Nohain, alias Jean-Marie Legrand, author of *Bonjour la France!*[11] was another prolific children's author. Among his other artistic activities, Nohain worked on the radio network during the war (*Radio-Nationale* in Marseilles), and with his brother Claude Dauphin, ran the travelling theatre company, the *Compagnie des Comédiens de France*. According to the Illustration of November 2nd 1940, the success of this company lay in its intrinsic Frenchness ('*c'est que les animateurs et le spectacle qu'ils donnent sont 100% français*'). As G. and J.-R. Ragache who report this accolade imply, this is probably not a press cutting Nohain would have cherished after the Liberation ('*Nationalisme un peu douteux à cette époque!*').[12] A similar 'nationalism' is to be found in the comic book *Benjamin*, founded in November 1929, in which Nohain was a principal collaborator, although this did not prevent Henri Coston from seeing in its title '*un nom bien juif qui prêtait heureusement à confusion*' [a thoroughly Jewish name that happily lent itself to misinterpretation].[13] *Bonjour la*

10. Dancette, V. and Jacques Zimmermann, *La Bête est morte. La guerre mondiale chez les animaux*, illustrations by Calvo, Editions de la Générale Publicité, 1945.
11. Jaboune [Jean Nohain], *Bonjour la France!*, poems by Christian Schwaebel, illustrations by Emmanuel Cocard, *Collection Tobby l'Eléphant*, Société d'Edition, façonnage, et impression, Villeurbanne, Presses Giraud-Rivoire, Lyon n.d., No. de censure OA 333.
12. Ragache, G., and J.-R., *La Vie quotidienne des écrivains et des artistes 1940-1944*, Hachette, 1988, p. 199.
13. Coston, H., op. cit., p. 22.

France!, prefaced by an extract from one of the *Maréchal*'s speeches,[14] clearly met with the approval of the authorities, for it received official clearance from the Vichy government, in the form of a '*numéro de censure*'.

Synopses

Il était une fois un pays heureux

This is the story of an idyllic country where climate and geography conspire to render its healthy and beautiful inhabitants the most envied in the whole world. A bad fairy, however, sows the seeds of madness in this happy community and the previously well-regulated citizens soon begin to show signs of complete degeneracy. Abandoning their rural idyll, the people move to the cities where they become absorbed in 'modern life' ('*une vie nouvelle qu'ils appellaient "vie moderne"*'), and, further encouraged by the advice of a number of 'strangers' or 'foreigners' ('*des étrangers*'), are blind to the negative effect their lifestyle is having on the previously fertile countryside and on the human population which declines rapidly as birthrates fall. Engrossed in their easy pleasures ('*plaisirs faciles*') the people fail to see the storm clouds of divine retribution gathering, and are powerless before the violent forces finally unleashed upon them. In the face of extreme meteorological adversity, including the raining down of fire and blood, the leaders of the people, many of them also foreigners, raised to preeminence by a bad fairy, counsel the continuation of the modern lifestyle. But above the babel of their foreign tongues is heard the calm voice of a patriarch, whose simple language speaks more eloquently to the most humble inhabitant. The advice He gives the people leads them back onto the path of righteousness and increased birthrates, and, with a new generation preparing to take up the challenge of the example He has set, the road they take is also the road to Happiness.

Six petits enfants et treize étoiles

This story tells of six children from varying social backgrounds, firm friends despite the envy and disdain that separate their parents. The children's favourite pastime is to visit the large wood near their village, where they are accepted by the animals and flowers who fear all careless and destructive grown-ups, with the exception of a solitary walker who lives somewhere deep in the wood.[15] One day, while playing in the wood, the children meet the solitary walker, who to their surprise knows all their names. He asks them in turn what they want to be when they grow up. The children answer, and he gives them advice about the virtues they should cultivate while achieving their career aims. When they part, the white-haired man gives the children permission to seek him out should they need his help, and this occasion arises some time later when the whole country is laid to waste by a tremendous storm. Separated from their parents, and from each other, the children follow the crowds fleeing from the destruction. When they finally meet, however, they decide to go against the flood of evacuees, and seek out the old man, and ask for his advice and help. Deep in the wood which has remained untouched by the storm, the old man responds to their appeal, and with one wave of his star-spangled baton, calms the storm. Taking individual stars from the baton, he throws

14. See the epigraph of this volume, p1.
15. As in *Il était une fois un pays heureux*, Pétain is never explicitly named in this story, but his identity is here made clear through reference to his traditional attributes (see section IV) and by one of the illustrations, which although portraying him only from the waist down, is easily recognisable because of the cut of the coat and trousers and the cane he carries, identical to those featured in a host of full-length drawings and photographs of this period.

them to the ground, and where they fall, farming implements, tools and seeds appear. These he gives to the three boys, and to the three girls he gives a cooking range, dressmaking equipment and a model farm. Two weeks later when the old man visits, the farm is prospering and as the months go by, the village comes back to life. The children thank the old man for his gifts, but he tells them that they hold the key to their own success. Gathering the children together, he instructs them each to hold the hand of the next as they had done in their moments of greatest adversity, and as François, Rose, Anne, Noël, Clément and Estelle all join hands, they spell out the name of their homeland - the most beautiful name in the world.

Bonjour la France!

This is the tale of Tiburce Bontemps and his younger sister Monique, who live in the charming little market town of Coucy-les-Bois. While Monique is good and sweet, a true little French girl ('*une vraie petite Française*'), Tiburce is unbearably naughty. Not only is he rude to his parents and badly behaved at school, he laughs at his sister and her veneration of the map of France that she has pinned to the wall above her bed. One night, after he has been particularly wicked, Tiburce is sent to bed with no pudding, and scarcely has he closed his eyes than he hears a strange noise. Sitting up in bed, he sees the map of France growing before his very eyes and it continues growing until its mountains and rivers burst through the walls of the house and spread out as far as the eye can see. Realising that this is France taking her revenge, Tiburce cries out an apology, and, with that, the tumult around him calms and he finds himself in a beautiful garden in the company of a mysterious woman. Monique appears, and the woman takes the children on a breathtaking tour of the garden which she tells them is not only hers but theirs as well, and which comprises coalfields in the north, seaside and cliffs in the west, fertile vineyards in the south, a market garden in the centre etc. The children are stunned by the size and variety of the garden and the woman tells them that it would take more than their whole lives to visit every corner of their domain, and that beyond the garden itself they own even more lands, where palm trees wave and hundreds of thousands of mouths murmur the name of France. France, for it is she ('*car c'était elle*'), dries the children's eyes as they sob with the emotion of their discovery, and takes them to a mysterious little lodge in the woods, where she reveals even greater wonders in the form of all the artistic triumphs of the nation, the great feats of civil engineering, and the works of the great French inventors. The most awe-inspiring revelation, however, is saved until last, when France evokes the children's valorous forbears from the great Vercingétorix to the most humble farmer who took up arms in 1914. She tells them that their greatest treasure of all is to belong to such a brave and illustrious race. The children are discovered sobbing in their beds by Madame Bontemps as she draws the bedroom curtains the following morning. Misunderstanding the cause of their apparent distress, she comforts them and tells them to forget their nightmare, but the children know that their marvellous adventure was real, and from that day on,

Tiburce and Monique are the best behaved children in the whole of Coucy-les-Bois.

Analysis

The first striking feature to link two of these stories with the fairy tale genre are their titles themselves; the Dancette text could not state its literary allegiances more clearly, and Paluel-Marmont gives a suggestion of the magic that is to follow in the reference to stars in his title. Nohain uses a more complicated device to evoke the literary genre with which he wishes his story to be associated. *Bonjour la France!* opens with a prologue which takes the form of an unidentified narrator gathering together a group of children to whom he/she is going to recount the story contained in the '*bel album rempli d'images*' [beautiful album full of pictures]. The narrator addresses the children directly from the outset:

> *Bonjour Pierre!...Bonjour Jacques!...Bonjour Henri... Janine... Marie... Françoise... Bonjour tous les braves petits garçons et toutes les belles petites filles de France!... [...].*
>
> Hello Pierre! [...] Françoise... Hello all the good little boys and the pretty little girls of France!... [...].[16]

Directed as much to the real audience of the text, wherever they may be, as to an imagined group of children, the direct address and absence of inquit tags, coupled with the familiar tone of this introduction, create an impression of immediacy and orality that recreates the act of storytelling, and by association brings to mind the classic substance of such recitations - the fairy tale. Having established in our minds the oral tradition of story telling, of which the folk tradition is, perhaps, the oldest manifestation, direct allusions by the narrator in the course of this introduction to the existence of a written text (the 'bel album' referred to above), also evoke the fairy tale as literary genre, and as a tangible object in the form of a picture book.[17] This announces a preoccupation on the author's part with the textuality and intertextuality of his creation, which reaches a self-conscious and, in the context of this study, a significant climax at the end of the prologue when the narrator remarks of the story he is about to tell '*c'est presqu'un conte de fées* [...]' (it is almost a fairy story [...]).

Were the reader to be in any doubt, however, as to the literary genre to which these texts owe much of their inspiration, all three texts adopt the classic fairy tale opening to their narrative: '*Il était une fois* [...]' (Dancette, Paluel-Marmont) and '*Il y avait une fois* [...]' (Nohain). What follows these instantly recognisable opening gambits is also the classic stuff of fairy tales, the narrative being liberally larded with superlatives and hyperbole, and every noun being qualified by a very flattering adjective. Thus, the '*pays heureux*' [happy land] of Dancette's title and opening sentence is envied by the entire world ('*dont le monde entier enviait le bonheur*'), and the six paragraphs that follow (approximately 200 words) are entirely devoted to extolling the attributes that make the country so

16. No page numbers are given in this text.
17. This latter point is stressed in a lengthy digression which explains that the pictures in the book are especially for the enjoyment of the younger readers and that the older siblings must ensure that the pages are neither dirtied nor torn by their younger brothers and sisters.

worthy of this attention. This description is so rich in examples of the narrative techniques referred to above, that to quote selectively from it would be as lengthy as to reproduce the whole passage, and would not convey the full flavour of the idyll. No excuse is made, therefore, for reproducing this description in its entirety:

Il était une fois un pays heureux dont le monde entier enviait le bonheur.
Ses habitants vivaient aisément, dans un climat agréable, se nourissant des produits variés d'un sol riche qu'ils se plaisaient à cultiver.
Les hommes y étaient sains et vigoureux; la pureté de leur âme se lisait dans l'azur de leurs yeux, leurs femmes étaient belles et leurs enfants adorables.
Une campagne aux aspects multiples et toujours enchanteurs assurait l'abondance dans la qualité. Ainsi la chère était-elle exquise. Les mets les plus simples étaient délicieux; le vin le plus ordinaire semblait un Nectar.
Des villes charmantes qu'un harmonieux désordre avait semées tout au long de rivières pittoresques étalaient la fantaisie de leurs rues étroites et sinueuses. Chaque détour de ce dédale invitant à la flânerie révélait quelque trésor d'architecture. Car ce peuple qui aimait le travail et les plaisirs sains d'une bonne table, avait aussi du goût. Les moindres bourgades abritaient tout un monde d'artisans dont l'ingéniosité et le talent tiraient des merveilles des matériaux du pays et faisaient l'admiration de l'Univers.
La science y était enseignée avec éclat par des maîtres incontestés dont le savoir et les vertus ajoutaient encore à la gloire de ce peuple privilégié.
Des contrées les plus lointaines on venait visiter cet heureux pays qu'un merveilleux passé avait assez comblé de gloire pour qu'il pût travailler paisiblement à son bonheur, sans regarder au-delà de ses frontières.
Les années s'écoulaient ainsi dans la douceur et la joie de vivre.

Once upon a time there was a happy land, whose happiness was the envy of the entire world.
Its inhabitants lived comfortably, in a pleasant climate, eating the varied produce of a rich soil which they enjoyed cultivating.
The men there were healthy and vigorous; the purity of their souls could be read in the azure of their eyes, their wives were beautiful, and their children adorable.
A varied and ever-enchanting countryside ensured both abundance and quality. Thus the fare it provided was exquisite. The most simple dishes were delicious; the most ordinary wine seemed like Nectar.
Charming towns that a harmonious disorder had strewn all along the picturesque river, displayed their haphazardly arranged narrow and winding streets. Every corner of this maze encouraged the casual stroller, and revealed an architectural treasure. For this people who loved work and the healthy pleasures of good fare, also had taste. The smallest hamlets harboured a whole population of craftsmen whose ingenuity and talent worked marvels on the materials of the country and were the admiration of the Universe.
Science was taught there with great style by the very best teachers whose knowledge and whose virtues further added to the fame of this privileged people.
From the farthest countries they came to visit this happy land, which had been sufficiently covered in glory by a marvellous past to allow it to work in peace at its own happiness without looking beyond its borders.
Thus the years passed by, full of happiness and the joy of living.

Paluel-Marmont portrays an idyll of a slightly different nature at the opening of *Six petits enfants et treize étoiles*, in that he is intent on conveying the close friendship that links the six children of his title. The methods he uses, however, are essentially similar: '*On* n'aurait pu *trouver un groupe de camarades* plus unis, ni plus sympathiques. Jamais nul *ne les avait vus se quereller [...]*' (my emphasis) [You couldn't have found a closer or a friendlier group of chums. No one had ever seen them quarreling]. Nohain, in *Bonjour la France!*, employs the same kind of techniques; the market town the children live in is charming ('*charmant*'), the shops are plentiful, varied and welcoming ('*toutes sortes de boutiques avenantes*'), and the village square is a 'pretty little' square, the joint attributes '*joli(e/s/es) petit(e/s/es)*' being extensively employed in this story, emphasising the picture book quality of the objects, places and people they describe. The regular Tuesday market held in Coucy-les-Bois further contributes to this picture of rural perfection, with the use of the very active pronominal verb '*se tenir*' (literally 'holds itself') qualified by the adverb '*gaîment*' ('gaily') contributing to the impression that the village itself is an animate and joyful participant in the scene. In its most extreme form, the animation of non-sentient objects is part of the stock-in-trade of the fairy tale writer,[18] going far beyond the literary device of personification which merely describes an object in human terms, actually to endow an object with discernable human, or at least sentient, characteristics, and attributing to these a significant role in the plot (see below).

In the Dancette text, the idyll so lavishly created at the outset, serves above all to emphasise the misguided nature of the people who could allow such a country to fall into disrepair, and to highlight, by its perfection, the depths to which the nation subsequently descends, and the monumental achievement of the man who succeeds in rescuing the people from this abyss. As the apocalyptic nature of the disaster that strikes France is recounted and the messianic nature of the country's saviour becomes apparent, religious language and imagery takes over from the language and structures of fairy tale. Paradoxically this shift is ushered in by the first explicit reference to fairies to appear in the text, when after the tell-tale use of the imperfect tense of the verb '*sembler*' [appeared] in the ominous phrase '*Les peuples heureux n'ont pas d'histoire. Et celui-ci,* semblait *assuré d'un long avenir de paix*' (my emphasis), we are told '*Mais une fée mauvaise vint semer la folie*' (p. 5) [Nothing ever happens to happy peoples, and this people *seemed* assured of a long and peaceful future. But a bad fairy came and sowed madness among them]. The only subsequent references to the fairy world, in the remainder, and thus the major bulk, of the text, are scarce and essentially superficial. While the land is described as being '*enchantée*' [enchanted], there is no elaboration on this idea; the '*vent de folie*' is referred to again only once, as is the '*fée malfaisante*'. Such references do suggest a cursory attempt to continue a theme and a literary style that serve an important function at the beginning of the text, although it is clear that they have been superseded by other literary models subsequently, particularly the biblical.

18. See Delarue, op. cit., pp. 39-41.

The magic and fantasy of fairy tale play a much more integral part in the stories told in the other two texts considered in this section, and thus represent a much more consistent element in the structure of these tales. In both stories we find the journey that provides the underlying framework of many folk tales (cf Propp) while the repetition of events or actions that characterises the majority of such tales is also apparent in Paluel-Marmont's story, with the children twice entering the wood, and twice conversing there with the white-haired man. The man interrogates each of the six children in turn about their plans for the future, and six times he throws the stars from his baton to the ground to produce the gifts he gives to the children.

The succession of good and bad events or situations that characterises many fairy tales and the traditional 'happy ending' to be found in all of Perrault's tales except *Le Petit chaperon rouge*, are also evident in both of these stories. In *Six petits enfants et treize étoiles* the idyllic life of the children is interrupted by the disastrous effects of the storm, only to be replaced by a much enhanced form of idyll through the intervention of the old man. In Nohain's story, the potentially ideal lifestyle of the inhabitants of Coucy-les-Bois is perturbed by the troublesome Tiburce, who soon mends his ways, however, when properly introduced to Monique's beloved France. In addition to this essentially traditional structure, and to the build-up provided by the prologue, Nohain has introduced two further elements to the plot sequence and narrative structure of *Bonjour la France!* that highlight the more oneiric passages. While the portrayal of the market town is idealised, it remains essentially realistic, to the extent that the author is at pains to convince us of the real existence of Coucy-les-Bois: '*Vous connaissez sûrement Coucy-les-Bois? C'est un charmant petit bourg de 3500 habitants, entre Villeneuve et Châteauneuf*' [Of course you know Coucy-les-Bois, don't you? It is a charming little market town with 3500 inhabitants, situated between Villeneuve and Châteauneuf]. Close scrutiny of a map of France may fail to reveal the exact whereabouts of such a town in the above-named vicinity, but the important effect of this realism is to make the fantasy element of the central part of the tale more prominent. The 'hinge' between the two sections is clearly signposted: '*et c'est ici, mes enfants, que se passe l'événement le plus inouï qui soit jamais arrivé dans la vie d'un petit garçon de dix ans*' [And it is at this point, children, that the most extraordinary thing happened that ever occured in the life of a little boy of ten].

Such interjections on the part of the extradiegetic narrator and his ongoing 'dialogue' with his audience continue beyond the end of the story of Tiburce and Monique. Apart from reinforcing the moral lesson of the tale - that all young French children should love and honour their country - this serves, as already noted, to remind us of the textuality and the intertextuality of the work. In addition to the explicit comparison between this story and other fairy stories which appears in the Prologue, a further reference is made to the genre in the body of the story itself, when the mysterious woman's skirts are described as being '*pareilles aux jupes que portent les fées dans les contes*' [like the skirts that fairies wear in fairy tales] (p. 19).

The language and narrative techniques that characterise the opening of all three of these texts and which associate them all closely with the fairy tale, continue to make their presence felt throughout the entire length of the Nohain and Paluel-Marmont stories, consistent with the continuation of the magical element through to the end of each tale. To emphasise the superabundance of flowers and birds in the wood where the children play, for example, Paluel-Marmont lists each species by name, and when he evokes them a second time, repeats the list in the same terms and the same order - a technique which evolved with the oral folk tale. Superlatives again abound, particularly in *Bonjour la France!* which in the course of the narrative has '*les enfants les plus heureux*' [the happiest children] (p. 10), living in '*un des plus jolis bourgs*' [one of the prettiest market towns] (P. 11), being shown a vegetable garden that is not only '*le plus appétissant*' [the most appetising], but also '*le plus admirable que l'on puisse imaginer*' [the most admirable that one could imagine] (p.20). Further exhibits in the magical garden, include:

> *[...] les plus purs chefs-d'oeuvre, les poèmes les plus émouvants, les cathédrales les plus éblouissantes, les découvertes les plus sensationnelles, les inventions les plus incroyables.*
>
> [...] the purest masterpieces, the most moving poems, the most stunning cathedrals, the most sensational discoveries, the most unbelievable inventions (p.27).

Nohain also uses the classic technique of repetition, this time for dramatic effect, when he describes the map growing out of all proportion:

> *La carte de France que Monique avait accrochée au mur venait de tomber par terre et elle s'agrandissait, elle s'agrandissait, elle s'agrandissait démesurément...*
>
> The map of France that Monique had pinned to the wall had fallen to the ground and it was growing and growing and growing out of all proportion (p. 14).

Repetition, accumulation and hyperbole are also used to great effect by Nohain to emphasise the size and wealth of France:

> *Un cheval qui galoperait pendant des jours et des jours, pendant des semaines et des semaines et pendant votre vie tout entière, vous n'auriez pas fini de voir et d'admirer tous mes jardins, toutes mes vignes, tous mes champs de blé, tous mes petits bois, tous mes ruisseaux, toutes mes montagnes... Tant notre propriété est vaste, riche, puissante et féerique!*
>
> If a horse were to gallop for days and days, for weeks and weeks and for the whole of your life, you would not have time to see and to admire all my gardens, all my vines, all my corn fields, all my little woods, all my streams, all my mountains... so vast, rich, powerful and magical is our domain (p. 22).

and this pattern is immediately repeated in an equally impressive evocation of the colonial posessions of France (see Appendix 3).

The simplicity of the language used in this extract and in all three texts considered in this section, is consistent not only with the high level of repetition, and with the reading/listening skills of the audience, but also with the Manichean nature of the message to be conveyed. A comparison of the most frequently used adjectives in all three texts, reveals not only a striking similarity between the Paluel-Marmont and Nohain, but also the predeliction for extremes displayed by the authors of many fairy tales (see Fig. 1 — all adjectives are listed in their masculine, singular form, although this may not be the case in the text).[19]

Paluel-Marmont	Nohain	Dancette
petit	petit	heureux
grand	beau	fort
beau	grand	mauvais
blanc	bon	meilleur
bon	pur	abondant

Fig. 1: Most frequently-used adjectives

As the quotation from Nohain suggests, in its use of the adjective '*féerique*', the language of enchantment is used throughout the texts, often in a manner that in other contexts might pass unnoticed, for the terms used have passed into common usage and lost much of their original literal meaning. Both stories contain examples of such terms as: *émerveillement, merveilles, merveilleux (euse/es), émerveillé(e/s/es), enchantement, enchanté(e/s/es), fantastique(s)* etc.. Overt references to the fairy world help to restore such words to their full resonance. Paluel-Marmont in his evocation of the wood in which the children play, describes the babbling of a brook that is so melodious '*qu'on n'aurait pu dire si c'était l'eau qui chantait ou quelque fée invisible vêtue d'herbe et coiffée de mousse*' [that it was impossible to say if it was the water that was singing or some invisible fairy dressed in grass with a hat of moss] (p.3).

The word '*fée*' [fairy] features five times in the Nohain text, most notably with the explicit identification of the main protagonist as France: '*C'est presque un conte de fées, mais avec la plus admirable, avec la plus douce des Fées: La FRANCE...*' ['It is almost a fairy story, but with the most admirable, the sweetest of fairies: FRANCE]. This direct linking of France and the fictional fairy tale world has an important cognitive effect, for however the country is portrayed in fiction, it continues to exist as a geographical and political entity in the real world. By explicitly identifying France as an integral part of the enchanted world of the story, some of that enchantment rubs off on the France of the real world, and the story is 'nearly' a fairy story not just because of its conformity or otherwise to a literary genre, but as an indication of near perfection in the real world.

A judicious choice of proper nouns also sensitizes the reader to the enhanced relationship between signifier and signified. In the best tradition of Perrault and such creations as *Cendrillon* [Cinderella], *Barbe-Bleue* [Bluebeard], *Le Petit chaperon rouge* [Little Red Riding Hood], *Le Petit Poucet* [Tom Thumb], etc., the names of the protagonists are not arbitrary,

19. A similar listing of the most frequently used nouns in each of the texts elicits a lot of vocabularly specific to the particular allegory adopted in each tale, but also demonstrates some emphasis on the key tenets of the National Revolution. Dancette's text is the most overtly propagandist in this sense, with '*Peuple*' '*pays*' '*terre/sol*' and '*travail/effort*' featuring particularly strongly, along with '*plaisirs faciles*' - the greatest threat to the nation. For an interesting and entertaining quantitative study of the vocabulary used by Pétain in his *Appels et messages*, see Miller, G., *Les Pousse-au-jouir du Maréchal Pétain*, Seuil, 1975.

bearing a close link to a physical trait in their owner. Paluel-Marmont explains the significance of the names of his six children at the opening of his story (Noël was born on December 25th, Rose has cheeks the colour of that flower, Estelle is the bright star in her parents' life etc.), but these links are as nothing when compared to the greater significance of the initial letters of their names, revealed at the end of the story. The same technique is used, although not consistently, in *Bonjour la France!*; the family name of Bontemps appears significant in the context of their near-idyllic existence, as does the fact that the children's humble but contented grandfather should be named Felix. Like Tiburce and Monique themselves, their father Joseph does not appear to benefit from any enhanced significance to his name, but it cannot be chance that caused Nohain to endow the mother with the doubly-saintly maiden name of Jeanne Maréchal! Whatever the importance of individual words, however, the true spirit of enchantment cannot be pinpointed by the compilation of a concordance of lexical items, and the most fertile area of analysis in these stories is their use of magical devices and conventions as an integral part of setting, action, and theme.

As generations of fairy stories testify, the wood or forest is a particularly privileged centre of action in the European folk tale. While Delarue argues that it is the Germans who most favour this setting,[20] the French tradition is not without its examples (*Le Petit chaperon rouge, Le Petit Poucet, La Belle au bois dormant...*), and it is a device used by both Paluel-Marmont and Nohain. Despite setting the action of his tale in the town of Coucy-les-Bois, a wood does not feature in *Bonjour la France!* until the final pages of the story, when the children are taken to a little lodge '*pareil à ces petits pavillons de chasse que vous avez peut-être vus dans certaines forêts*' ['just like those little hunting lodges that you have perhaps seen in certain forests']. Although the forest itself is not described, the lodge serves the same function as the woodcutter's cottage, or the witches lair in a hundred other forest clearings - providing a moment of dramatic tension in the narrative, and a setting for magical encounters. When the children are taken to the mysterious little lodge ('*le petit pavillon mystérieux*') as the last and the most impressive stage in their whirlwind tour, it is there that all the most marvellous treasures of France are magically gathered together.

The enchanted forest plays a much greater role in *Six petits enfants et treize étoiles*, providing an important setting for much of the action, greatly contributing to the magical and idyllic ambiance, and providing important insights into the character and actions not only of the children, but, more importantly, of the white-haired man. The magical atmosphere of the woods is established by the reference to the fairy-like singing of the brook referred to above, the description of the marvellous light ('*une lumière si merveilleuse*') which pervades the wood despite the thickness of the overhead foliage, and through the personification of the flowers and animals who shrink at the sight of adults, but who do not fear the children or the solitary walker (thus establishing an important connection between the old man and the untainted virtues of youth). Later on, when the storm has devastated the entire countryside, the wood remains untouched and

20. Delarue, op. cit. p. 36

is, as ever, bathed in '*cette lumière enchantée*' [this enchanted light]. In the best traditions of the fairy tale there is an anthropomorphic animal (or bird in this case - a robin) on hand to add to the magical atmosphere, and the choice of adjective to describe this bird, described as a '*rouge-gorge familier*' gives it obvious associations with the witch's familiar, the '*démon familier*'.

Personification and anthropomorphism are central to *Bonjour la France!*, with the reader first having a foretaste of the magical transformation that is to occur, when Monique imagines that her map of France looks like a human face, whose facial/geographical characteristics are described in some detail. Soon afterwards, the map really does come to life in a fantastic kind of earthquake, and whilst it retains its vegetable and mineral nature, it is endowed with human emotions, for as Tiburce realises, it is taking its revenge on his scornful behaviour towards it. In confirmation of this, the earthquake calms as he cries out his apology and in a further transformation, becomes a tranquil and beautiful garden. While the animal, vegetable and mineral qualities of France are now represented by this beautiful garden, the spirit of the nation is embodied in the mysterious woman, whose sudden appearance in the garden, like Monique's, is all part of the enchantment. Directly referred to at one stage as '*la fée mystérieuse*', the sylph has all the qualities that mark her out as a member of the fairy godmother sorority. In the true tradition of such characters, she is slightly disguised when she first appears, taking on the features of a beautiful, if rather mysterious, woman. She is betrayed, however, by the greying hair which frames her young face - a clear indication of her links with eternity. Her magic powers enable the children to travel for many hours without tiring, and her knowledge and patience are boundless.

Omniscience is a quality shared by both Nohain's mysterious woman and the old man in *Six petits enfants et treize étoiles*. Nohain's France is familiar with the life of Tiburce and Monique's grandfather, Felix Bontemps, as well as the entire history of the nation, while Paluel-Marmont's character knows the names of all the children when they first meet in the forest. The white-haired gentleman's talents as a magician go far beyond such a simple trick, however, for armed with his *maréchal*'s baton in the guise of a magic wand, he is able to effect the kind of magical transformation of which any self-respecting fairy godmother would be proud. The 13 stars that feature on a French marshal's baton are perhaps the original inspiration behind the adoption of the fairy tale genre as the governing force in this story, and they certainly come into their own in the dramatic climax to the tale. In the best tradition of Perrault, internal realism is maintained even at the height of magical activity, for while some of the gifts the white-haired man gives the children are conjured up by the stars out of thin air, others are transformed from everyday objects, such as a pile of wood and metal debris, which becomes a blacksmith's forge. There is a direct parallel here with the magical transformations effected in *Cendrillon* [Cinderella], where not only is a similar technique used, but where the objects and animals/people conjured up bear a significant physical resemblance to the objects from which they were transformed (silver-skinned lizards become footmen dressed in silver brocade; a fat, bewhiskered rat becomes a tubby coachman with a magnificent moustache etc.). To crown his efforts, the old man effects the ultimate magical transformation, by himself disappearing into thin air: '*Et brusquement, à la place où il se trouvait, il n'y eut plus personne, sans que nul ait pu voir comment ni de quel côté il avait disparu.* [And abruptly, in the place where he had stood, there was nobody, without anyone being able to say either how or where he had disappeared to] (p. 21).

If the internal realism of such tales conforms to the standards set by Perrault and his literary descendants, the coherence of the allegory is also well-managed, and above all, appears remarkably faithful to the true spirit of Perrault in terms of dénouement. In keeping with the aspirations of the supporters of the real-life Maréchal, the white-haired gentleman of Paluel-Marmont's tale does effect a miraculous transformation in the ravaged country, but, as the miracle-worker himself is at pains to point out, the secret of the nation's rebirth is in each of its inhabitants -'*le secret de votre réussite est en vous*' [the secret of your success is in you] (p. 24). Similarly, in *Bonjour la France!*, the most important message that France teaches the children amidst the incredible size and fertility of their dominions and the amazing inventions and discoveries of their countrymen, is that their greatest riches come from within:

> *Elle [votre plus douce richesse] ne se voit pas avec les yeux, elle ne se touche pas avec les doigts... Elle est dans votre tête, dans votre coeur, dans chaque goutte de votre sang. Elle est dans votre beau regard si pur et si net.*
>
> It [your sweetest treasure] cannot be seen with your eyes, it cannot be felt by touch... It is in your head, in your heart, in each drop of your blood. It is in your fine expression, so pure and so clear (p. 27).

While Perrault would argue that it is human nature, not magic that is ultimately at the root of everything we achieve and experience, however, the propagandist is more partisan. Intrinsic qualities may play their part in the golden future of these young people, but the overriding arbiter of their internal configuration is their heredity, their membership of a favoured race, '*une race de braves gens simples, courageux, travailleurs...*' [a race of good simple people, brave, hardworking...] (Nohain p. 27). The same message is to be found in *Six petits enfants*: as Paluel-Marmont's six children join hands, they finally understand the full significance of the old man's message:

> *Alors nos six petits amis comprirent qu'avec ces six lettres ils allaient pouvoir composer un nom très beau, un nom si beau qu'il est en effet le plus beau de tous les noms, le plus noble, le plus généreux, le plus gonflé d'espérance...*
> *Et ils murmurèrent avec ferveur:*
> *- FRANCE.*
> *... le nom de leur Patrie bien aimée.'*
>
> Then our six little friends understood that with these six letters they would be able to compose a beautiful name, a name so beautiful that it is actually the most

> beautiful of all names, the most noble, the most generous, the one most full of hope...
> And they murmured fervently:
> - FRANCE
> ... the name of their beloved Fatherland (p. 24).

If Philippe Pétain, in his mid 80s, is not the classic stuff of fairy-tale heroes, his advanced years, combined with his heroism at Verdun, mean that he is well-suited to the role of sage counsellor and worker of strong magic depicted in stories such as those of Dancette and Paluel-Marmont. In such tales, physical characteristics of the living man are transformed into the identifying emblems of a new Pétain, who becomes part saint, part deity, part fairy godfather as his essence is distilled and purified with each wave of the author's pen, a latter-day magic wand. As in the creation of the settings and events portrayed in these stories, reality is enhanced to create a larger-than-life image of the Saviour of the nation; the detailed descriptions of the idyllic country and its apocalyptic downfall giving credence and logic to the superhuman qualities displayed by the leader who can rescue such a catastrophic situation and restore the nation to its former glory. Despite the obvious associations between the '*patriarche*' in Dancette's story, '*l'homme aux cheveux blancs*' in Paluel-Marmont's tale, and the leader of the *Etat français*, however, Pétain is never explicitly identified in either text. These anonymous figures thus remain fictional creations, among a host of other fictional characters, events and settings, benefiting from the more liberal margins of behaviour and achievement that fictional, particularly magical, status allows. The miraculous acts performed by these superheroes may ultimately be essentially allegorical, but to the naive reader, the impressive quality of the fictional actions remains firmly anchored in the imagination. Anonymity and thus fictionality may allow such acts to be portrayed, but by ensuring that the real leader of the nation is associated by very strong implication with these superhuman creations, the authors nevertheless ensure that Pétain gains in status from the marvellous actions of his fictional alter egos.

But if the real man could be transported into the land of fiction in order to enhance his reputation, so, the propagandists found, the language and techniques of fiction could be used to enhance ostensibly non-fictional accounts for children of the great man's life. The resulting 'stories', discussed in the next section, often read more like the charmed adventures of some mythical superman, than factual biography of a military and political leader. If the ultimate effect of this technique is hagiographic, with all that that term implies of religious language and imagery, the narrative structures and language of the fairy tale also contribute to the creation of the quasi-mythical being who is to save the nation a second time. Physical and psychological descriptions of the *Maréchal* in later life benefit most extensively from the use of such techniques, although, as the propagandists were quick to realise, Pétain's early life and his rise to national preeminence were not without their affinities to the origins and fortunes of many a folk hero, a factor that has important implications for the overall narrative structure of the texts.

IV
'Once upon a time, there was a *Maréchal* of France...'

The Cult of Pétain

The particular veneration of which Pétain was the object between 1939 and 1943 is the subject of numerous studies, many of which are listed in the Bibliography of this volume. As Girardet has demonstrated, focusing public attention on one charismatic figurehead is a standard propaganda technique. It is no surprise, however, that Girardet should have chosen to illustrate the cover of his book *Mythes et mythologies politiques* (Seuil, 1986) with an illustration of Pétain, so numerous were the visual representations of the *Maréchal* produced under the *Etat français*. Even less surprising is the fact that this picture is taken from an album for children, as children represented the largest target audience for such memorabilia.

The wide variety of different images of the *Maréchal* produced in a number of different media, combined with the huge numbers into which many of the more popular editions ran,[1] demonstrates the vital role played by iconography in the propaganda initiative designed to acquaint, or re-acquaint the nation with their new leader. Photographs, drawings and even statues all served to render the physical appearance of Pétain familiar throughout the land, and with the aid of careful manipulation by the propagandist, many of these images also succeeded in conveying some of the intrinsic qualities of the man and his mission. By portraying the *Maréchal* in his uniform, they evoked, not the disastrous events of the recent *débâcle*, but the glorious military career of the hero of the First World War, who having saved the day at Verdun, would now guide the nation through its darkest days to a golden future in a New Europe. This golden future was also portrayed symbolically in many portraits of Pétain, by the simple expedient of superimposing his image on that of a rising sun. Similarly, it was a simple matter to depict the rural origins of the *Maréchal* and to suggest his continuing affinity with the land and its people, by picturing him shaking the hand of a farmer as the peasant pauses awhile in his ploughing to wipe the honest sweat from his brow (see illustration overleaf). Above all, the portraits of Pétain capture the direct gaze of his blue eyes, mirroring the purity of his moral integrity, and his clear vision of France's future.

While pictures could do a great deal, however, (and the examples sketched out above are only a small proportion of the visual possibilities for symbolism exploited by the propagandists), text also provided a number of opportunities for enhancing the *Maréchal*'s reputation, the favoured medium for the younger audience being a highly simplified form of biography. This format, like Pétain himself, found favour in both the southern and northern zones of France, as the bibliographical

1. A poster featuring Pétain's head and shoulders, in military uniform against the French flag, designed by Philippe Noyer in 1940, entitled *Révolution nationale*, had a first print run of 510,000 copies in unoccupied France, with a second edition of 550,000 copies in 1941. A reproduction of this poster, and details of many of the other images of the Maréchal produced during this period can be found in the lavishly illustrated publication: Gervereau, L., and Peschanski, D., (eds), *La Propagande sous Vichy 1940-44*, Collection Publications de la BDIC, 1990.

'La Terre, elle, ne ment pas', Imageries du Maréchal, Limoges, 1941.

details below demonstrate. These details also suggest that, unlike the iconography of the period which emanated from a limited number of official sources (such as the *Imagerie du Maréchal* referred to in Section I), these biographies were not necessarily directly commissioned by the Vichy government.

Case Studies

Origins

With the exception of Paluel-Marmont, already referred to in the previous section and author of two books more specifically about the *Maréchal*, few biographical details are available about the other children's authors and illustrators who chose to focus on the life of Philippe Pétain. Of the four authors whose works are referred to here, Paluel-Marmont is the one who has the most obvious links with the Vichy régime (see Section III). One of his biographies of Pétain, entitled *Il était une fois un Maréchal de France*, was sold as part of the '*Noël du Maréchal 1941*' organised by the Secours National as part of their winter aid scheme, the '*Entr'aide d'hiver du Maréchal*' (see illustration opposite). This scheme was launched for the first time on 11th November 1940 by Pétain himself, and involved the collection of clothes and money as well as the sale of books, in aid of French prisoners of war in Germany, and the poor. The company responsible for actually printing this text, Curial-Archereau of Paris, was a prolific source of children's books during the Second World War, both pro-Vichy propaganda and non-politicised escapism,[2] and continued to operate after the Liberation, when it printed, among other works, an appreciation of General de Gaulle,[3] and a pro-Resistance adventure story, *Disque Rouge*.[4] Paluel-Marmont's second study of the *Maréchal*, simply entitled *Pétain*, published in 1942, was also published and printed in

2. The *Bibliographie de la France* and the catalogue of the children's library in Paris, the *Heure Joyeuse*, though certainly not an exhaustive record, list 21 books produced by this printing house during the period 1942-45.
3. Anon, *Le Général de Gaulle*, Paris, Hachette, 1945.
4. Vincent, P., *La Belle aventure du Disque Rouge*, Illustrations by Gad, Imprimerie Curial-Archereau, Paris, 1945.

Paluel-Marmont, A., Il était une fois un Maréchal de France, illustrations by Pierre Rousseau [and Germaine Bouret], 'Edité par Fanfan la tulipe, journal pour enfants', les Editions et Publications Françaises, Imprimerie Curial-Archereau, 1941.

Paris, this time for the 'Librairie des Champs-Elysées' (director Albert Pigasse) on the presses of a company called Blanchong. The book itself includes full details of every individual that played a hand in its production from engravers to suppliers of paper, and records the production of a special copy destined for Pétain himself '*en fervant hommage des artisans de ce livre: l'auteur, l'illustrateur, l'éditeur, les graveurs, imprimeurs et brocheurs*' [in fervent homage from the makers of this book: the author, the illustrator, the publisher, the engravers, the printers and the binders].

The three other texts discussed in this section were all published outside Paris, although one, *La Vie d'honneur du Maréchal Pétain racontée et illustrée pour les jeunes français*, text and illustrations by Pierre Herault

[1940], was also produced in occupied territory, by Farré et Freulon in Cholet (Maine-et-Loire). *La Vie du Maréchal Pétain racontée aux enfants de France*, by Roger Descouens [1940] was published in the unoccupied southern zone, by the Editions de la Vraie France in Nice, on the presses of the *Eclaireur de Nice*. Also from the south came *La Belle histoire d'un chêne*, by Yvonne Estienne, produced by the Editions de la Revue *'Les Alpes'*, Grenoble (1942). Both Descouens' and Estienne's works were approved by the censor in Vichy prior to publication, receiving an official '*numéro de censure*' which was printed on the cover of the book. *La Belle histoire d'un chêne* also lists a series of censor's numbers for the pictures it contains.

Analysis

Starting, in the best storytelling tradition, at the beginning, it is the opening of these biographies of Pétain that firmly establish the mythical qualities of their subject. All of these texts, from the outset, deliberately set up a series of resonances and expectations in the young reader's mind, concerning the kind of story that they are about to read. The cover illustration of Hérault's *La Vie d'honneur du Maréchal Pétain*, executed, like all the illustrations in the book, by the author himself, is a fine example of the symbolic portrayal of the leader of the *Etat français*. Pétain's distinctive features, topped by military kepi, gaze out of the page, while behind this noble yet approachable figure, a brilliant sun rises over the fields and haystacks of the French countryside (see illustration opposite). This visual reference to Pétain's role as Saviour of the Nation (the rays of the rising sun *almost* appear as a halo around the *Maréchal*) is taken up by both Hérault and Paluel-Marmont (in *Pétain*) in the opening phrases of their books. Both adopt the technique used by writers of the ostensibly non-fiction form, the historical exemplary life, to endow their hero with mythological status and near-sainthood through association with such legendary figures as Vercingétorix, Bayard and Joan of Arc (see Section I). While such characters have achieved legendary status over a period of many centuries, the modern hero is able instantly to benefit from the same kind of veneration through identification with these noble figures. Hérault explicitly likens Pétain to Joan of Arc, designating both as the kind of exceptional or miraculous beings who periodically come to the aid of the Nation in its hours of greatest need, while Paluel-Marmont pens an exceptionally lyrical tribute to Pétain and his forbears in patriotic valour:

> *O mon pays, je veux chanter l'Homme qui t'a conservé la vie, l'émule de Bayard le Chevalier et le disciple de Jeanne la Très Sainte, comme lui sans reproche et sans peur et comme elle portant l'armure de la Foi.*
>
> Oh my country, I want to celebrate the Man who has saved your life, emulator of the Knight Bayard and disciple of the saintly Joan, like him blameless and fearless, and like her, wearing the armour of Faith.[5]

Paluel-Marmont also uses this technique in *Il était une fois un Maréchal de France*,[6] but both he and Descouens adopt an even more clearly signposted

5. There are no page numbers in this text.
6. '*Il s'appelait Philippe Pétain. Mais jamais on ne le nommait ainsi. Comme on eût dit Vercingétorix ou Pasteur, on disait : Pétain, simplement*'. [He was called Philippe Pétain. But no one ever called him that. As one would have said Vercingétorix or Pasteur, one said simply: Pétain.]

Hérault, P., La Vie d'honneur du Maréchal Pétain racontée et illustrée pour les jeunes français (text and illustrations), Farré et Freulon, [1940].

fictional model for their work, and a different kind of mythical identity for Pétain in the opening of their biographies, through the use of the classic '*il était une fois*'. Any narrative which begins in this manner is deliberately exploiting a series of pre-conditioned responses in its readers. The indeterminate temporal setting of such a narrative, with its intimations of timelessness, strongly argues for the mythical nature of the actors involved. Familiarity with other examples of the genre leads to anticipation of the creation of an atmosphere of enchantment, in which superhuman acts are natural, not to say *de rigueur.* To begin a biography in such a manner is thus a very clear attempt to elevate the subject to the enchanted plane and this incursion into the world of fiction is the very basis of the propagandist's art, for it is through association with the marvellous, (its characters, stories, formal structures and vocabulary) that Pétain is elevated to apparently superhuman status in the eyes of the young reader. Paluel-Marmont sums up this metamorphosis in his conclusion to *Il était une fois un Maréchal de France*:

> *Sa vie est aussi claire et lumineuse qu'une légende. Et c'est pourquoi, lorsqu'on veut la conter, on commence ainsi que nous avons commencé ce livre: "Il était une fois un Maréchal de France...".*
>
> His life is as clear and luminous as a legend. And that is why, when one wants to relate it, one starts just as we began this book: "Once upon a time there was a Marshal of France...".

Both Descouens and Paluel-Marmont consolidate the effect created by this classic opening phrase through their continuing use of both the narrative structures and the essential story-line of a number of fairy stories in their opening pages. Descouens echoes the traditional opening of the majority of Perrault's tales, not only with the classic 'Once upon a time', but with another technique often used by Perrault, that of linking this opening to a direct introduction of the social status of the family and the number of children it contains. Descouens' tale begins: '*Il était une fois un cultivateur qui, déjà, avait trois enfants*' [Once upon a time, there was a farmer who already had three children]. Compare this with *Le Petit Poucet*, '*Il était une fois un bûcheron et une bûcheronne qui avaient sept enfants, tous garçons* [...]' [Once upon a time there was a woodcutter and his wife who had seven children, all boys [...]]; *Cendrillon*, '*Il était une fois un gentilhomme qui épousa, en secondes noces, une femme [...] Elle avait deux filles [...] le mari avait, de son côté, une jeune fille*' [Once upon a time there was a gentleman who was married a second time, to a woman [...] She had two daughters [...], on his side, the man had a young daughter]; *Les Fées*, '*Il était une fois une veuve qui avait deux filles*' [Once upon a time there was a widow who had two daughters]; *Riquet à la houppe*, '*Il était une fois une reine qui eut un fils* [...]' [Once upon a time there was a queen who had a son [...]], etc..

In order to emphasise the universal applicability of his tales, Perrault avoided giving any names to the kingdoms, forests, towns or castles in which the main action of his stories occurs (similarly the names of the protagonists, as we have seen, are highly symbolic, representing types rather than individuals). The authors of Pétain's biography are keen to link their subject to a specific place in France, not only to validate the theme of his authentic rural origins, but also to help all the young readers identify with this man who comes from a small village very much like their own. The name of Pétain's birthplace is, however, particularly suited to the fairy-tale atmosphere these authors all seek to create, for Cauchy-la-Tour has the kind of rhythm and lyrical resonances that are particularly fitting to the genre (cf Coucy-les-Bois, the name Nohain chose to give the town featured in *Bonjour la France!*). If this were not enough, Descouens transforms the name slightly to become Cauchy-à-la-Tour, an even more sing-song title, which also serves to bring the tower, a recurring architectural feature in fairy tales, into particular prominence. Both Hérault and Paluel-Marmont reinforce the rhythmic qualities of the name of the village by immediately following it with the similarly hyphenated name of the *département* where this village is to be found: the *Pas-de-Calais*. This repeat rhythmical and visual pattern bears some resemblance to the formulaic use of repetition and rhymes in Perrault, referred to in Section II.

In *Il était une fois un Maréchal de France*, Paluel-Marmont builds on his title and his opening line with another classic fairy tale technique, that of giving a physical introduction to the main character. In fairy tales, such characters are all, of course, either supremely beautiful/ handsome/ good or monumentally ugly/ proud/ wicked, their appearance often having important consequences for the way in which those around them subsequently behave. This presentation of cause and effect is introduced on a number of occasions in Perrault by the construction '(subject) (verb) *si* + (adjective), *si* + (adjective) que ...', the use of the adverb '*si*' serving the dual purpose of intensification and causality. *La Belle au bois dormant* [Sleeping Beauty] begins in the following manner:

> *Il était une fois un roi et une reine qui étaient si fâchés de n'avoir point d'enfants, si fâchés qu'on ne saurait dire.*
>
> Once upon a time there was a king and a queen who were so cross that they had no children, more cross than one could possibly describe.

Riquet à la houppe [Riquet with the tuft] begins thus:

> *Il était une fois une reine qui eut un fils si laid et si mal fait, qu'on douta longtemps s'il avait forme humaine.*
>
> Once upon a time there was a queen who had a son so ugly and so deformed, that for a long time people wondered whether he was really human.

In *Les Fées* [The Fairies], the construction is extended to cover two sentences:

> *Il était une fois une veuve qui avait deux filles [...]. Elles étaient toutes deux si désagréables et si orgueilleuses, qu'on ne pouvait vivre avec elles.*
>
> Once upon a time there was a widow who had two daughters [...]. They were both so disagreeable and so proud, that they were impossible to live with.

Paluel-Marmont reproduces this structure in his presentation of Pétain:

> *Il était une fois un Maréchal de France dont l'allure était si noble, le regard si droit, la voix si douce que tous - faisant plus que l'admirer - l'aimaient, et que même ceux qui avaient été ses adversaires le tenaient en haute estime.*
>
> Once upon a time there was a Marshal of France whose bearing was so noble, his gaze so direct, his voice so gentle that everyone - more than admiring him- loved him, and even those who had been his enemies held him in high esteem.

The same technique, enhanced by a high incidence of repetition, is used later on to portray his valour:

> *Si raides fussent les pentes à escalader, si étroits les sentiers jonchés de rocailles sur lesquels on n'avançait que d'un pas mal assuré, si traîtres fussent les ponts de neige qu'on devait franchir pour passer d'un glacier à un autre, si mordant fût le froid, si violente la tempête, toujours il marchait à leur tête [...].*
>
> However steep were the slopes to be climbed, however narrow the stony paths along which one only advanced with great caution, however treacherous the bridges of snow by which one passed from one glacier to another, however biting the cold, however violent the storm, he always marched at their head[...].

At the beginning of Paluel-Marmont's and Descouens' accounts of the *Maréchal*'s life, it is in the role of the classic folk hero that Pétain seems destined to appear, and their adoption of the folk medium is no arbitrary choice in relation to the actual events in Pétain's life. Latter-day Marquis de Carabas (*Le Chat botté*), he comes from humble rural origins, and although lacking a helpful feline companion, rises to the political equivalent of marrying the beautiful princess, as sole commander of the *Etat français*. The similarity does not end here, for in the manner of a fairy tale, history repeats itself several times in the course of Pétain's career. In retelling and stressing the successive appeals that the nation makes to Pétain (World War One, Morocco, Spain, World War Two) and his repeated willingness to come to the aid of the patrie, all of Pétain's biographers are reproducing the kind of plot structure found in many fairy stories and creating many of the same kinds of effect as a result. Even Hérault, who does not explicitly adopt the fairy tale mode, emphasises this recurring pattern, not only in Pétain's own life, but in the history of the nation. He describes in some detail the different military and diplomatic situations in which Pétain is involved in the First World War, Morocco and Spain, stressing at each stage Pétain's devotion and obedience to the needs of his country, despite the poor treatment he receives at the hands of the politicians and other military men of the Third Republic and the Popular Front. This recurring pattern reminds us of the opening sentence of the book, which, evokes an eternal and miraculous version of the same process:

> *Qu'y a-t-il donc d'écrit dans le destin de notre Patrie pour que, chaque fois qu'elle semble devoir mourir, surgisse de son sol un être exceptionnel ou miraculeux?*
>
> What is there written in the destiny of our Mother Country that means that each time she seems destined to perish, she brings forth an exceptional or miraculous being from her soil?

Turning away from the more obvious points of comparison with the structures and narrative forms of the fairy tale, many of the other literary devices used in fiction in general, and the fairy tale in particular, find their way into these ostensibly factual biographies, contributing to the creation of a larger-than-life persona for the *Maréchal*, and a very magical quality to the acts he performs. Reference has already been made to the hyperbolic detail used in the portrayal of fairy tale characters, and as we have seen, such a device is used in Paluel-Marmont's initial portrayal of Pétain in *Il était une fois un Maréchal de France*. This trend is reinforced subsequently by the description of Pétain as a child: *'fort de muscles, prompt d'intelligence, ardent au travail, généreux de coeur'* [strong of muscle, quick of mind, willing worker, generous of heart], and the suggestion of almost excessive perfection finds an unconscious echo in the reference to the '*centaines de milliers*' [hundreds of thousands] of Frenchmen who have been under his command. Although perhaps true, this figure is the kind of unspecific huge number used by children to conjure up a quantity beyond their wildest imagination.

Physical description has another important role to play in propaganda texts. Concentration on certain distinctive physical traits, through which a person is characterised both physically and psychologically, is not a technique unique to the fairy tale genre, but is certainly a staple of such tales as *Barbe-Bleue, Cendrillon, Le Petit Poucet* etc., as the very titles of such tales indicate. In the majority of Perrault's tales, this emphasis on *être* and *paraître* is taken a step further, when the relationship between external appearances and true identity is brought to particular prominence. In Perrault, external disguises are often diametrically opposed to the intrinsic qualities of those who affect them, a good fairy appearing as an ugly old hag, for example (*Les Fées*). Appearances can be altered in different ways, not only by the waving of a magic wand (as in *Cendrillon*), but also by simply effecting a minor change in apparel: in *Le Petit Poucet*, the ogre is fooled into eating his own children when the hero switches the nightcaps worn by his own brothers with the gold crowns worn by the ogre's offspring. All the wolf has to do to trick Little Red Riding Hood, for a while at least, is to slip into Grandma's bed, and disguise his voice slightly.

The authors of the books studied in this section make comprehensive use of the technique of emblematic identification, Pétain being designated most frequently by facial characteristics (hair, eyes, moustache), 'psychological' traits (his sparing and considered use of language), and symbols of his military rank (kepi, baton). The use of the designated emblems goes beyond the evocation of the living man through metonymy, to symbolise more fundamental metaphysical attributes. Thus, in these stories, there is never any question of physical appearance being a form of trickery, but rather the concentrated essence of the virtues of the inner man.[7] This technique is used both in the fictional stories discussed in Section III, and in the ostensibly non-fictional biographies discussed here.

The recurrence not only of the same technique, but of the very same emblems in both sets of literature undoubtedly helps further to blur the distinction between reality and fantasy, real and mythical characters, in the young readers' minds. In *Six petits enfants et treize étoiles*, the children are impressed by the tall stature, the serious face and the white hair of the solitary walker, who is afterwards referred to, in a very Perrault-esque manner, as '*l'homme aux cheveux blancs*' ('the white-haired man'), the colour white being here a sign not only of his venerable age, but also of his moral purity. Even Pétain's moustache is given a particularly patriotic significance by Hérault and Paluel-Marmont, who describe it as being both '*à la française*' and '*à la gauloise*', the latter perhaps also

7. In Dancette's *Il était une fois un pays heureux* it is language that is seen as a great source of trickery, not physical appearance, so Pétain, with his simple, direct, language stands out among all the other political leaders who seek deliberately to mislead the people through their fine speeches.

encapsulating an encoded reference to the omnipresent Vercingétorix!

As we have already noted, the eyes are always one of the most striking features in visual representations of Pétain. They are also often commented on in literary references to the *Maréchal*, both through descriptions of their appearance (clear, blue, piercing, etc.), and their faculty for looking into the inner thoughts of his interlocutors. In *Six petits enfants et treize étoiles* two famous 'trademarks' of the *Maréchal* are joined in the description of the audience the old man gives to the six children:

> *Il parlait d'une voix très calme, un peu grave, sans hâte, en donnant aux mots tout leur sens, et en regardant dans les yeux celui ou celle à qui il s'adressait.*
>
> He spoke in a very calm voice, quite deep, slowly, giving each word its full meaning, and looking straight at the boy or girl he was talking to.

This sparing use of language is highlighted by all three authors who link it to his fundamental moral integrity which also characterises the simple and transparent nature of his rare utterances. In Hérault, this taciturn immovability finds physical expression in Pétain's near-metamorphosis into the very rock of his native land ('*Ce n'est presque plus un homme, c'est un roc sorti de la terre de France*'), while Paluel-Marmont places him even higher as '*l'aigle sur un roc céleste*' [the eagle on a celestial rock] (*Pétain*).

Metaphor is not only used in descriptions of Pétain, it is also used to portray events, the most common example of this being the use of the image of a violent storm to portray the First and Second World Wars, an image employed by all of the authors discussed here and in the previous section, with the exception of Nohain who does not set *Bonjour la France!* within the context of the War. If this storm metaphor may appear somewhat hackneyed through over use, its presence in the Vichy propagandists' panoply of literary devices is justified on special grounds. In addition to the classic points of comparison between wars and storms (storm clouds gathering, the rumble of thunder/cannon fire, rain/bullets raining out of the sky, etc.) the portrayal of the Second World War as a natural phenomenon had the particular advantage of obviating the need to blame the war on any external aggressor, i.e. the Germans. The absence of any explicit or even veiled reference to the Nazis in any of these stories is not a concession to the censor, but a genuine desire to overlook the transgressions of the country's new partner in the New Europe, and an apparently genuine belief that it was not ultimately the Germans who were responsible for the nation's downfall.

The personification of France that forms the basis of Nohain's *Bonjour la France!* also features in Paluel-Marmont's *Pétain* when the country calls on Pétain to help abroad in the colonies and in Spain. This image is further developed in *Il était une fois un Maréchal de France*. Here, as in Nohain's tale, France is characterised as a woman, but rather than being the mysterious and beautiful fairy in control of her own destiny, she has become '*une grande dame imprévoyante*' [a highborn lady lacking in foresight] who calls on Pétain '*son sauveur habituel*' [her habitual saviour] to come to her aid when a tornado devastates the beautiful castle she has inherited from her forbears, and which she has allowed to fall into serious disrepair.

The importation of such essentially literary techniques into factual biography reaches a climax in the allegorical identification of Pétain as a mighty oak tree. Again this is a device used both in the biographical and the 'fictional' representations of Pétain. While it features as one simile among others in the fictional stories, however, it stands out more clearly in the ostensibly non-fiction texts, introducing an element of fantasy through the anthropomorphisation of the tree, and through the corresponding elevation of Pétain from mere mortal to superhuman being, part man, part oak, endowed with the very best qualities of that noble tree. The most outstanding example of this technique, is Yvonne Estienne's *La Belle histoire d'un chêne.* In this story, not only are the impressive physical attributes of the tree described, but the oak is personified as a leader, a king, a fearless protector of the other forest plants and animals. Having opened her story with a picturesque account of how the noble tree protects the entire forest against the onslaughts of a violent storm (a real one in this instance), Estienne uses the increasingly familiar storm analogy as a transition to the Second World War. It is interesting to note, however, that, although the war is introduced in this allegorical manner, as 'another storm', the description that follows is one of the most realistic evocations of the armed conflict to appear in children's books of this period, not least because of its direct appeals to the personal experience of the young readers:

> *Les mamans avaient dû abandonner leur maison et toutes les jolies choses qu'elle contient; elles s'enfuyaient sur les routes avec les plus jeunes d'entre vous enroulés dans une couverture ou traînés dans leur petite voiture... Et l'on avait faim! Est-ce que vous ne vous souvenez pas de ces jours où l'on a été si malheureux?...*
>
> The mummies had had to abandon their houses and all the lovely things in them; they were fleeing along the roads with the youngest of you rolled up in a blanket, or pulled along in a little cart...And everyone was so hungry! Don't you remember those days when everyone was so unhappy?...

The Germans may not be mentioned by name in this story, they feature only as '*l'adversaire*', but the realities of the hurried exodus from occupied territory are dramatically portrayed, and the pictures that accompany this section of the text are not only realistic, but they contrast markedly with the other idealised and allegorical illustrations that accompany the rest of the text. The remainder of the book is essentially factual in nature, but the allegorical connection between Pétain and the oak is made explicit: '*Et le grand beau chêne s'appelait le Maréchal Pétain*' [And the handsome great oak was called Maréchal Pétain] and the forest analogy is maintained, if unevenly to the end of the book. This is achieved through the simple, if somewhat bizarre technique, of sporadically inserting the characters of the initial fable into the factual account in the latter part of the text, giving a strange mixture of the two modes. Thus the Maréchal (in his fully human form) addresses the nation in its allegorical disguise as '*la forêt*' [the forest], and more specifically, '*les brins d'herbe piétinés*' [the trampled blades of grass]. Meanwhile, factual details concerning Pétain's biography are given the title '*Le Passé du Grand Beau Chêne*' [The History of the Handsome Great Oak].

The relationship between Pétain and his sylvan emblem becomes all the more complex when the essentially poetical devices of personification and anthropomorphism are integrated into a real life event involving oak trees. At the end of the book, Estienne recounts the ceremony held to dedicate an oak to Pétain in the forest of Tronçais (one of many such events that were held during this period). As Pétain enters the wood (the classic site for enchantment...), the trees recognise him as their brother:

> Les grands arbres du bois reconnaissent le Maréchal pour leur frère, ils se montrent les feuilles de chêne qu'il porte à son képi.[8]
>
> *The great trees of the wood recognize the Maréchal as their brother, they point out to each other the oak leaves on his kepi.*

In the dedicatory address, the youth and vivacity of the 270-year-old oak is likened to Pétain's continuing sprightliness: '*il est toujours jeune et vivace comme vous*' [it is still young and hardy like you], and the statistical details about the immense height and girth of the tree, and its illustrious history and remarkable survival all serve to give the tree a magical quality which is transfused into the man to whom it is likened and whose name it will bear.

Unfortunately for Pétain and his eulogists, the political influence of the ageing *Maréchal* was not as long-lived as the mighty oak, and the latter months of 1942 began to see a perceptible decline in the fortunes of the *Révolution nationale* and its figurehead. Although Pétain's personal popularity persisted beyond the end of the war, his political credibility and usefulness effectively ended with the Allied invasion of North Africa and the resulting occupation of the southern zone. The *Maréchal* remained the nominal head of the *Etat français*, but effective power was transferred to Laval, and the heyday of Vichy propaganda was over.

8. The kepi of a French marshal is decorated with a band of golden oak leaves (see illustrations).

V
The Impact of Children's Propaganda and Broader Implications

Assessing the Impact of Propaganda

The continuing popularity of Pétain — he was mobbed by ecstatic Parisians on a visit to the capital in 1944 — suggests that in this area at least, Vichy propaganda made a lasting impression. It would be naive, however, to attribute such a phenomenon solely to the efforts of the propagandists. In monitoring the evolution of public opinion, particularly in times of national crisis, there are many other factors that play a part in influencing popular conduct and beliefs. Studies in Germany, repeated at regular intervals throughout the Second World War, have been able to demonstrate the evolution of public opinion in that country in a number of significant areas, but while they appear to make a strong case for the influential properties of propaganda, the evidence is ultimately inconclusive. To take but one example, according to these studies, a clear progression can be charted in public perception of the Jewish community in Germany, moving from initial indifference, to an increasingly negative and fearful attitude, which ultimately leads to widespread acceptance of Hitler's so-called 'final solution'. This evolution in public opinion appears to follow closely the increasingly violent and radical message being transmitted through the medium of propaganda. While acknowledging the important role played by propaganda in this area, however, one cannot discount other factors that may have influenced public opinion in this regard; factors such as the military fortunes of Germany as the war progressed, notably the defeat at Stalingrad (February 1943) and the national sense of shock and vulnerability that resulted. More prosaic but equally influential were domestic considerations, a shortfall in supplies encouraging a more hard-hearted attitude to rivals for the small amounts of food, clothing and fuel available.

If the Germans conducted similar studies in France, the *Lageberichte* which were produced every month from August 1940 to April 1944, these reports should also be treated with caution, not least because they themselves constituted a form of propaganda through which their authors sought to influence their masters in Germany. Nevertheless, as Thalmann points out, these reports do confirm the initial success of the *Révolution nationale* and the continuing popularity of Pétain, two fundamental strands in Vichy propaganda, although they also chart a growing reaction against anti-Semitic measures and the propaganda that accompanied them (including the violent film *Der Juden Süss*), and a growing anti-German sentiment that does not directly result from any form of official propaganda campaign and indeed runs counter to the general thrust of Vichy, and of course, German propaganda.[1]

But if these studies are inconclusive as regards the importance one can attribute to propaganda in determining public opinion among the adult population, they have nothing to say about the younger children addressed by the kind of propaganda discussed in this study. While the *Lageberichte* follow the progress of the multitude of quasi-military organisations available to the teenage population of France, and report on the measures taken to exclude the Jewish community from the Universities and the teaching profession, no mention is made of the pre-adolescent and his or her reaction to the contemporary situation, international or domestic, let alone to the kind of propaganda of which they were a target. Other contemporary sources are equally disappointing in this respect. A collection of essays written by schoolchildren in the village of Tournissan in the Languedoc between 1939 and 1945,[2] concentrates exclusively on the material hardships experienced during this period. Whether as a result of the parameters established by the exercise itself, or of a process of selection operated by the editor, Rémy Cazals, no reference is made in these touching narratives to any extra-curricular, or indeed curricular, reading that may have influenced the opinions of these pupils. Certainly no influence of the fairy tale style is evident in the very factual descriptions of rationing and occupation that these valuable eye-witness accounts provide.

Further study of contemporary archives, particularly the work of school children, may eventually provide some evidence of the effect of Vichy propaganda on its young audience, or at the very least some indication of the percentage of the population actually exposed to this literature. At present, there is little to indicate the level of penetration achieved by the kind of texts discussed in this volume. Although details of print runs and sales cannot provide any kind of compelling proof as to the impact of the message a book may contain, such information can at least point to the popularity, however transitory, of a given work. Just as bibliographical details of children's books during the war are woefully lacking, however, so too are figures concerning their production and distribution; a result both of lack of archival evidence, and the neglect hitherto experienced by this branch and period of French publishing history. Some scant details about print runs are provided by the texts themselves, but as in the example given in Section III (*Il était une fois un pays heureux*) these only tend to refer to special numbered editions, and not to the copies produced for more widespread general consumption.

If contemporaneous evidence is insubstantial, can we assemble any valid data from memories recalled by adults who were part of the pre-adolescent generation in the period 1939-1945? Autobiographical memory is a notoriously difficult area of study, where personal recollection, never guaranteed infallible at the best of times, may be influenced by a number of different factors, not least the subsequent course of historical events. These difficulties are exacerbated when the period under recall is that of Vichy France, a great many French adults today, as at the Liberation, refusing to admit that they may have been

1. Thalmann, R., *La Mise au pas. Idéologie et stratégie sécuritaire dans la France occupée*, Fayard, 1991, pp. 73-128.
2. Cazals, R., (ed.) *Les Ecoliers de Tournissan 1939-1945*, Privat, 1978.

supporters of the *Maréchal* and his *Révolution nationale*, others excusing or explaining a 'temporary lapse' with any number of forms of justification. Those who fell into the pre-adolescent category in the Second World War might feel more justified than others in admitting today to having read, even to having enjoyed, Vichy propaganda, their naivety and vulnerability to parental pressure absolving them of any contemporary or subsequent complicity with the régime and the beliefs and policies it advocated. To date, no such study has been made, although Jill Sturdee, in collecting childhood recollections of Occupation in Caen,[3] has incidentally recorded some data relating to comics during this period. The results of her inquiries in this area might at first appear disappointing: of the small sub-set of 15 informants whom she questioned more particularly on this topic, only two had any recollection of seeing Vichy-orientated comics, and then only on the news stands (one recalled *Le Téméraire*, the other, *Fanfan la Tulipe*). As superficial (and potentially revisionist) as such memories may be, however, if this proportion of 'positive' results were to be reproduced in a larger sample-study, over a wider geographical area, a useful pattern of the distribution and penetration of such publications might begin to emerge.

The Adult Reader

If it is difficult to assess whether Vichy propaganda for children did indeed reach its target audience and make any impression, lasting or otherwise, on their young minds, reference to the role of the parent in overseeing a child's social, moral and political education leads us to question whether children were indeed the only target of the kind of propaganda material discussed in the previous sections. As mediators between children and the literature to which they are exposed, parents inevitably come into contact with the content of children's propaganda. In purchasing, or approving the purchase of literature, parents have a superficial contact with the content and style of a work, and, for the age group with which we are concerned, this contact is consolidated by the process of aiding the child in reading the text, or of completely taking over the function of transmission. Each of these functions necessitates not only exposure to the text, but active participation in its conveyance to the young audience, and this involvement is particularly marked in tales related to the folk genre whose origins lie in the oral tradition. Depending on the curiosity of the young audience and the didactic/political zeal of the adult involved, reading will probably also include a degree of interpretation of the political message contained in such works.

Of all the texts discussed in this study, the biographies in Section IV are probably the ones that have the most immediate contemporary political relevance for the child reader and which might require the least explanation on the part of a parent. As we have seen, the name and image of Pétain was so omnipresent in French life at this time, that no one, not even the primary school child, could ignore his identity and political role. The stories discussed in Section III might have less immediate contemporary significance to the young reader, particularly as all references to the war and the character of Pétain himself are shrouded

3. Sturdee, J., 'Children of the Occupation: An Analysis of the Effects of the Nazi Occupation Upon the Children of Caen, Summer 1940 - Summer 1944', thesis in progress (University of Sussex).

in allegory, but their overall themes, of patriotism, national unity and moral rectitude are integrated into the 'plot' to such a degree that they cannot be ignored by even the most naive audience. In case of extreme inattention on the part of adult or child, Nohain has incorporated into his narrative a clear pointer to the contemporary relevance of his tale, not only by placing an extract from one of Pétain's speeches as an epigraph to the story but with the words '*vous tous qui venez de lire cette histoire* vraie' (my emphasis) [all of you have just read this *true* story] in the concluding paragraph. Here, the juxtaposition of '*histoire*' and '*vraie*' acts as a clear signal for the informed reader that they are in the presence of allegory if not of political myth-making.

The same technique is used by the anonymous authors of *Doulce France et Grojuif* and *L'Homme aux mains rouges*, tales in which the fictional events described are sufficiently coherent and entertaining to be accepted without reference to their political interpretation, although divergences from the original models should awake the curiosity of the child audience. The anti-semitic text declares its contemporary relevance from the outset with the uncompromising declaration which appears on the first page: '*"Le petit Chaperon Rouge" n'est qu'un conte, mais "Doulce France et Grojuif" est une histoire vraie qu'il faut lire!*' ["Little Red Riding Hood" is only a tale, but "Sweet France and Fatjew" is a true story that must be read!]. *L'Homme aux mains rouges* ends with a similar statement, concluding: '*Et voilà terminée, l'histoire merveilleuse et* véridique *de l'HOMME AUX MAINS ROUGES.*' (my emphasis) [And that is the end of the marvellous and *true* story of THE MAN WITH RED HANDS]. Adults might, therefore, be called upon to explain the contemporary relevance of these tales, and to provide the key to each of the features that differentiate these stories from their beloved and probably highly familiar originals. Within each text, there is also plenty of scope for an adult to enhance the effect desired by the authors. *Doulce France et Grojuif*, already an 'interactive' story like the Perrault original thanks to the question and answer session at the end, offers further potential for amateur dramatics with the phonetic spelling of Grojuif's responses designed to aid the reproduction of a supposedly Jewish accent. In *L'Homme aux mains rouges*, an adult has many opportunities for introducing a more factual explanation of France's relationship with Stalinist Russia, while identification of the recurring motifs semi-hidden in the illustrations could provide an entertaining introduction to the state's iconography.

To what extent such texts may actually have been intended for adult as well as child audiences is open to debate. Of all the children's books referred to in this study, only the *abécédaire* alluded to in Section II makes an explicit connection between the two audiences, in its subtitle '*à l'usage des petits enfants qui apprennent à lire et des grandes personnes qui ne comprennent pas encore le français*' [for young children learning to read and for grown-ups who don't yet understand French]. Of the texts studied in detail, it is the fairy tale parodies of Section II that appear most likely to have been designed with this dual function in mind. This hypothesis is corroborated in part by the wider political knowledge needed correctly to interpret the contemporary allusions, but arises also from the very genre itself, which traditionally contains mechanisms designed to address and involve the adult reader just as much as a young audience. As we have suggested (see Section II) the adult reader might be expected to discern 'hidden' messages even in the classic tales of Perrault.

Over and above the adult allusions contained in the literary fairy tales of the 17th century, a strong argument in favour of ascribing a wider audience to the fairy tale propaganda is the historical fact that traditional folk tales were originally destined for adult audiences. These oral tales were only subsequently orientated towards a younger audience, partly as a result of the efforts of Perrault and his successors, and even then remained a staple of peasant culture through the eighteenth and nineteenth centuries.[4] Renonciat gives details of a French edition of the Grimms' fairy tales which appeared between 1911 and 1929, and comments that the publisher, Piazza, '*a publié un grand nombre de volumes de contes, luxueusement illustrés et* destinés tout autant aux adultes qu'aux enfants' (my emphasis) [published a great number of volumes of tales, luxuriously illustrated and *destined as much for adults as for children*].[5] Even without the support of such historical credentials, Lüthi would argue that adults are naturally drawn to reread the fairy tales of their youth at certain periods later on in their lives,[6] and one might argue that in a period of crisis, such as the Second World War, recourse to such tales, comforting not only in their familiarity, but also in their traditional 'happy ending', might be all the more likely.

In analysing the wide appeal of the fairy tale, Soriano characterises the link that the fairy tale has exploited between children and the peasant classes from the 17th century onwards, as being '*l'ignorance et la crédulité*' [ignorance and credulity].[7] This connection also seems to have been an important factor considered by the Vichy propagandists when formulating tactics for targeting specific sections of the population. Faure comments on this connection with regard to visual propaganda, remarking that: '*si l'image influence ainsi l'âme enfantine, elle n'influence pas moins l'âme populaire qui est d'une fraîcheur analogue*' [If pictures thus influence the soul of the child, they have no less an influence on the popular soul, which is of a similar purity].[8] Laurence Bertrand Dorléac refers to '*la naïveté souvent rurale*' [the often rural naivety] of a lot of Pétain memorabilia,[9] confirming this perceived link between peasant and infantile innocence, and laying the stress particularly on the agricultural nature of the peasantry in France. Dorléac also comments that the need to educate this natural simplicity in the correct manner entailed '*la nécessité d'existence de messages simples et répétitifs, instruments de consolidation du pouvoir par l'image*' [the need for the existence of simple and repetitive messages, instruments of the consolidation of power through the image].[10] In the visual arts, this perception of a large section of the adult population is translated into the mass production of *images d'Epinal*, the very simplistic, pastel coloured, wood-cut style pictures produced by the *Imagerie du Maréchal* - the visual equivalent of the fairy-tale style in literature. It may have been that what is ostensibly children's fiction was actually aimed equally at the significant rural population that still existed in France at this time who,

4. Kramnick, op. cit., p. 213 and Soriano, op. cit., pp. 340-345.
5. Renonciat, A., *Livre mon ami: lectures enfantines 1914-54. (Catalogue établi et rédigé par Annie Renonciat)*, Mairie de Paris, 1991, p. 43.
6. Lüthi, op. cit., p. 22.
7. Soriano, op. cit., p. 340.
8. Faure, op. cit., p. 171.
9. Dorléac, L. B., 'La Question artistique' in Rioux, J.-P. (ed), *La Vie culturelle sous Vichy*, Complexe, 1990. p. 150.
10. Ibid.

although their levels of literacy had risen significantly since the nineteenth century, might still be expected to favour the traditional literature of their class.

The influence of children's literature on the propaganda of Vichy France goes beyond this suggestion that some adults may have come into contact with material primarily destined for children. It is unnecessary perhaps to point out that the simplified narrative structures and lexical range that typify children's literature are well suited to propaganda aimed at any age range. Miller has, however, provided convincing proof that such simplicity typifies Pétain's public speeches delivered between June 17 1940 and April 18 1942.[11] More fundamental than this, as we have suggested, the ideal world of Fairy Land inspired the very conception that many propagandists and politicians, including Pétain himself, had of *la nouvelle France*, in turn then providing the only form in which such a vision could be adequately expressed.

Thus we find not only the adoption of thematic and stylistic elements more commonly found in children's literature by authors writing for adult audiences, but more particularly many features very closely associated with the fairy tale. An excellent example of this premise, is the work of René Benjamin, a well-known admirer of the *Maréchal*, whose ostensibly non-fiction book for adults, *Le Maréchal et son peuple*,[12] has much in common not only with the idealised biographies for children (Section IV), but also with the fictional stories discussed in Section III. A long extract from this book, gives a flavour of the style, with its simple grammatical structures and relatively unsophisticated vocabulary, and also demonstrates the use of very similar idealised settings and identikit characters to those which feature in the children's stories, particularly the early scenes portrayed in *Bonjour la France!*. In theory at least, however, this is an eye-witness account of a real visit that the Maréchal has made to a small town in France, '*une petite ville française*' - complete with the diminutive that invariably describes such settings in fiction and which appears as the most frequently-used adjective in the tales of both Nohain and Paluel-Marmont (Section III, fig 1).

> *Il était très tôt. Un train de nuit m'avait déposé là à la pointe du jour. J'étais seul sous le ciel rose, où se promenait un dernier quart de lune. Je me disais, en sortant de la gare, que je devais être le premier levé. Mais je n'avais pas fait trois pas que j'apercevais dans les boutiques des lampes allumées et des ombres humaines, qui frottaient qui rangeaient, qui achevaient une devanture. On voyait partout le portrait du Maréchal, partout des fleurs et des rubans aux trois couleurs, avec l'inscription : "Vive la France!" [...]*
> *Pourtant, des volets restaient encore fermés. Ils ne le furent pas longtemps. Ils s'ouvrirent d'une façon charmante et imprévue, aux sons d'une aubade que vinrent donner sur les places une douzaine de clairons, commandés par un officier. Douze soldats alertes, avec des instruments astiqués, qu'ils faisaient d'abord tourner prestement dans leurs mains gantées de blanc, de beaux gants à crispins. Puis, ils embouchaient, et en quelques notes vives ils tiraient du lit les dormeurs, les prévenant que c'était jour de fête! [...] Le Maréchal était en route, il approchait;*

11. Miller, G., *Les Pousse-au-jouir du Maréchal Pétain*, Seuil, 1975.
12. Benjamin, R., *Le Maréchal et son peuple*, Plon, 1941.

il arrivait! Avant que la fanfare eût cessé, les volets s'étaient ouverts; on voyait les gens en chemise se frotter les yeux, sourire à la vue des soldats et du ciel clair, et déjà ils criaient: "Vive Pétain!"
Un coup de clairon ici, un autre là, de place en place, de rue en rue, la ville en un rien de temps fut éveillée. Il n'était pas encore sept heures : les ménagères se pressaient chez le boulanger, chez l'épicier, pour ne pas être en retard. On voyait des scouts se hâter en bouclant une dernière courroie. M. le Président du Tribunal se trouvait sur la place de l'Hôtel de Ville dans sa tenue des grands jours, jaquette et pantalon rayé, serrant dans une main ses gants neufs. Le maire, dans la même tenue, sortit en hâte, courut vers lui, et d'une voix empressée ils dirent ensemble: "Nous avons tout le temps!.."
Les soeurs de Saint-Vincent-de-Paul groupaient déjà les enfants. Ce sont d'admirables mères poules. De leurs robes à plis et de leurs vastes cornettes elles recouvrent tous leurs poussins. Chaque écolier tenait son petit drapeau. C'était, collée le long de sa règle, une belle feuille du cahier, coloriée par lui. Les soeurs ont un sens divin de l'économie dans le bonheur. Toute leur troupe piaillait de joie.
Les vieux n'étaient pas moins empressés. Ils avaient déjà pris place au bord des trottoirs. On leur disait: "Va donc te reposer encore. On te garde ta place." Ils faisaient: non. Le Maréchal lui, se reposait-il? Ils prétendaient être aussi jeunes que lui. Et ils voulaient être au premier rang pour le remercier de leur avoir donné une retraite.
Enfin, j'allais chercher le sous-préfet. Il essayait des gants de peau blanche, éclatants. Il me dit en les admirant:
— La mercière n'a jamais voulu que je les paye. Elle m'a dit, les larmes aux yeux: 'Me payer! Pour le Maréchal!' Puis, elle a ajouté: 'Quelle chance vous avez, avec ces gants-là, de lui serrer la main! Je ne vous demande qu'une chose: pensez à moi!' [...]

It was very early. A night train had set me down there at daybreak. I was alone beneath a rosy sky, where you could still see a crescent moon. As I left the station, I thought to myself that I must be the first one up. But no sooner had I taken three steps, than I saw lights on and the shadows of people polishing and tidying, and putting the finishing touches to window displays. Everywhere you could see portraits of the Marshall, everywhere flowers and tricolor ribbons with the inscription 'Long Live France!' [...]
And yet there were some shutters still closed. But not for much longer. They were opened up in a charming and unexpected way, to the sound of a reveille played by a dozen buglers, commanded by an officer. Twelve smart soldiers, with their brightly polished instruments, which first of all they twirled nimbly in their hands, hands that were clad in beautiful white gauntlets. Then they put their instruments to their lips, and with a few lively notes they pulled the last sleepers from their beds, telling them that it was a day of celebration! [...] The Marshall was on his way, he was getting closer; he was arriving! Even before the fanfare had ended, the shutters were open; you could see people who had just got dressed rubbing their eyes, smiling at the sight of the soldiers and the clear sky, and already they were shouting 'Long Live Pétain!'
The sound of a bugle here, another there, from square to square, from one street to another, in no time at all the whole town was awake. It wasn't yet seven o'clock: housewives were rushing to the butcher's, to the grocer's, so as

> not to be late. Scouts were hurrying, buckling their belts. The Chief Magistrate could be seen in front of the Town Hall in his ceremonial jacket and striped trousers, clutching a new pair of gloves. The mayor, similarly attired, came rushing up to him, and they both gasped: 'We've got plenty of time!...'
> The Sisters of St Vincent de Paul were already organising the children. They are splendid mother hens. With their flowing robes and ample cornets they enveloped all their little chicks. Each pupil held a little flag; his own ruler with a hand-coloured sheet of paper attached to it. The nuns have a great sense of economy in the midst of celebration. The whole batch was squawking with excitement.
> The old people were just as keen. They were already stationed along the pavements. People said to them: 'Go and have a rest. We'll keep a place for you.' But they said no. Does the Marshall rest? They claimed to be as young as he was. And they wanted to be there in the front row to thank him for giving them a retirement pension.
> Finally, I went to find the *sous-préfet*. He was trying on some brilliant white kid gloves. As he admired them, he said: 'The haberdasher wouldn't let me pay for them. She said to me with tears in her eyes: 'Pay me! For the Marshall!' Then she added: 'How lucky you are, with those gloves there, to shake hands with the Marshall! I only ask you one thing: think of me as you do it!' [...]

This extract encapsulates a number of the important propaganda themes associated with Pétain; the close identification of the *Maréchal* and his country (his portrait is surrounded by tricolor flags, the townspeople cry 'Vive la France' and 'Vive Pétain' indiscriminately), Pétain's remarkable vigour, and above all his role as Saviour of the Nation - a touch of his hand, even through gloves, takes on the equivalent value of a holy relic. It also reproduces some of the symbolism most frequently used by the propagandists of the *Révolution nationale*, - the importance of the colour white, the significance of a clear sky. What is particularly remarkable about the passage, however, is the atmosphere that is created; that of a brightly coloured Toytown, peopled by figures whose only identity is their profession, distant cousins perhaps of 'Mr Bun the Baker' and 'Mr Plod the Policeman', etc. of *Noddy* fame. The model village even has a complete set of toy soldiers, all neatly turned out in their identical uniforms, putting their shining bugles to their lips with the precision of clockwork... And just like some of the more complex cutting-out books designed by the *Imagerie du Maréchal* — open the shutters and look at the people rubbing their sleepy eyes.

In promoting the circulation among adults of stories characterised by their naive tone and idyllic images, the government was seeking to influence the broadest possible audience, who were to be seduced not only by the ideological content of such stories, but, more insidiously, by the very form that they took. Children, as we have seen, are central to the political and ideological conception of the *Révolution nationale*, but childhood itself is also a potent symbol for the propagandists of Vichy France. The children who people the stories of Nohain and Paluel-Marmont are themselves symbols of the innocent and trusting faith that *all* the population should place in Pétain; their untainted souls allowing them a privileged relationship with the natural world and the very spirit of their country, a relationship that their parents have forfeited under the accretions of age and 'modern life'. The evocations of a pre-war Golden Age, an age of innocence that existed before the advent of the Popular Front and the temptations proferred by exotic foreigners, this also is a reminder of the joys of childhood, both individual and collective. Above all, however, the topos of childhood is fundamental as a reminder of the paternalist relationship between Pétain and the Nation, and these books themselves are a symbol of that relationship. The stories may be designed to sell the Golden Age myth, the conspiracy theory, or the image of a new saviour, but the story book form was designed to place the adult reader firmly in the role of acquiescent and submissive child.

The image of an expectant group of children grouped around a father or grandfather figure, the kind of scene evoked in the opening of *Bonjour la France!*, is a metaphor for the nation grouped around its leader, magically present in every home through the medium of the wireless. Having been reproved for their bad behaviour in the past, and admonished to be good in the future, they listen in obedient silence to the *appels* and *messages*, to the measured tones, the simple language, the familiar and cherished formulae. They listen to the reassuring voice telling them about the golden future of a country with a golden past, of 'once upon a time' and 'happy ever after'; they listen to Pétain telling them ... fairy stories.

Appendix One

PRIMARY SCHOOL TIMETABLE (1941)

Premier cycle

	Heures		
Matières	Section prépara-toire.	Cours élémen-taire.	Cours moyen.
Education morale, civique et patriotique	1	1	1
Lecture	9	6	3
Ecriture	4	2	1.5
Langue française	2.5	5.5	6.5
Histoire et géographie		2	2.5
Calcul	2.5	3	4
Sciences	1	1	2
Dessin. Travail manuel à l'intérieur et en plein air	2	1.5	1.5
Education physique et chant	3	3	3
Plein air	3	3	3
Hygiène pratique	0.5	0.5	0.5
Récréations	1.5	1.5	1.5
Total des heures d'enseignement obligatoire	*30*	*30*	*30*
Instruction religieuse (facultative)	1.5	1.5	1.5
Totaux	**31.5**	**31.5**	**31.5**

Source : Ozouf, R., *Le Nouveau statut de l'école et du personnel enseignant primaire. Recueil de documents officiels*, Editions FN, [1941]

EXTRACT FROM THE SYLLABUS

Education Morale, Civique et Patriotique

Premier cycle

I. Section préparatoire

Morale

Causeries morales : récits historiques destinés à faire naître chez l'enfant la piété envers la patrie.

(une heure par semaine)

II. Cours élémentaire

Education morale et patriotique

Entretiens familiers sur des sujets moraux ou historiques empruntés à la tradition nationale ou locale.

Etude de pages à valeur éducative empruntées aux monuments de la langue française : moralistes, écrivains politiques, messages du Maréchal Pétain.

La patrie; l'attachement au sol natal; le respect de la famille.

Les forces morales et leurs sources spirituelles.

(une heure par semaine)

III. Cours moyen

Education morale et patriotique

Lectures et entretiens; les devoirs de la vie sociale; le respect du travail et des travailleurs; la famille; la société; la patrie. Les vertus individuelles; la conscience, l'amour de l'effort; l'esprit de sacrifice; le courage; la bonté et la tolérance; la tempérance; la modestie; la sincérité.

La tradition et l'unité françaises.

La civilisation chrétienne.

(une heure par semaine)

Source : Ozouf, R., *Le Nouveau statut de l'école et du personnel enseignant primaire. Recueil de documents officiels,* Editions FN, [1941]

Appendix Two

PARALLEL PRESENTATION OF *DOULCE FRANCE ET GROUJUIF* AND *LE PETIT CHAPERON ROUGE*

Doulce France et Grojuif Anon	***Le Petit chaperon rouge***[1] Charles Perrault
Il était une fois une bien gentille petite fille nommée "Doulce France".	Il était une fois une petite fille de Village, la plus jolie qu'on eût su voir;
Toute sa famille l'aimait tendrement et sa grand'mère "Vérité" l'adorait.	sa mère en était folle, et sa mère-grand plus folle encore.
Cette bonne "Vérité" lui fit faire une coiffe rouge qui lui seyait si bien que partout on l'appelait "le petit chaperon rouge".	Cette bonne femme lui fit faire un petit chaperon rouge qui lui seyait si bien, que partout on l'appelait le Petit chaperon rouge.
Un jour, sa mère ayant préparé[2] des galettes succulentes lui dit:	Un jour sa mère, ayant cuit et fait des galettes, lui dit
-Va voir comment se porte ta grand'mère Vérité.	-Va voir comme se porte ta mère-grand,
Il paraît qu'elle est souffrante.	car on m'a dit qu'elle était malade,
Porte-lui des galettes et ce petit pot de beurre.	porte-lui une galette et ce petit pot de beurre.
Doulce France partit aussitôt.	Le petit chaperon rouge partit aussitôt pour aller chez sa mère-grand,
Sa grand'mère habitait une gentille maisonnette tout près d'une grande-forêt.	qui demeurait dans un autre Village.

1. This is the text of the first edition of the tale (excluding the *moralité*), and exactly reproduces the capitalisation and punctuation of the original. Only the layout has been changed, to facilitate a comparison with the propaganda version.
2. This version 'corrects' Perrault as do many editions of the original tale, misunderstanding the intransitive use of the verb 'cuire'.

Chemin faisant, Doulce France rencontra soudain le loup Grojuif surgissant des fourrés.[3]	En passant dans un bois elle rencontra compère le Loup,
Il eut envie de manger aussitôt la belle petite Doulce France,	qui eut bien envie de la manger;
mais il n'osa le faire, craignant les braves bûcherons qui travaillaient dans la forêt.	mais il n'osa, à cause de quelques Bûcherons qui étaient dans la Forêt.
Grojuif se fit gentil et demanda au Petit Chaperon Rouge où elle allait.	Il lui demanda où elle allait;
La bonne petite fille qui ne savait pas que Grojuif était dangereux à écouter,	la pauvre enfant, qui ne savait pas qu'il est dangereux de s'arrêter à écouter un Loup,
lui répondit: - Je vais voir ma mère'grand "Vérité".	lui dit: - Je vais voir ma Mère-grand,
Elle est malade et je lui apporte des galettes avec un pot de beurre.	et lui porter une galette avec un petit pot de beurre que ma Mère lui envoie.
- Demeure-t-elle loin? questionna Grojuif.	- Demeure-t-elle bien loin? lui dit le Loup.
- Oh oui!	- Oh! oui,
dit Doulce France: c'est la belle maison que vous voyez tout là-bas, derrière la lisière du bois.	dit le petit chaperon rouge, c'est par-delà le moulin que vous voyez tout là-bas, là-bas, à la première maison du village.
- Eh bien! dit le loup, je veux l'aller voir aussi.	- Hé bien, dit le Loup, Je veux l'aller voir aussi;
Moi je prends ce sentier et toi,	je m'y en vais par ce chemin ici,

3. The villain appears in a much more sudden and frightening manner in this version.

passe par ce chemin-là.	et toi par ce chemin-là, et nous verrons qui plus tôt y sera.
Grojuif, bien qu'ayant pris le chemin le plus court, se mit à courir de toutes ses forces.	Le Loup se mit à courir de toute sa force par le chemin qui était le plus court,
Doulce France, confiante,	et la petite fille s'en alla
	par le chemin le plus long,
s'amusa à cueillir des noisettes, à courir après les papillons et à faire des bouquets de fleurs.	s'amusant à cueillir des noisettes, à courir après des papillons, et à faire des bouquets de petites fleurs qu'elle rencontrait.
Le loup ne fut pas long.	Le Loup ne fut pas longtemps à
Il arriva à la maison de la mère'grand et heurta l'huis:	arriver à la maison de la Mère-grand; il heurte:
Toc! toc!	Toc, toc.
- Qui est là?	- Qui est là?
Déformant sa voix, Grojuif répondit: - C'est votre petite-fille, Doulce France,	- C'est votre fille le petit chaperon rouge (dit le Loup, en contrefaisant sa voix
qui vient prendre de vos nouvelles et vous porter quelques friandises.	qui vous apporte une galette et un petit pot de beurre que ma Mère vous envoie.
La bonne "Vérité", clouée dans sont lit par la maladie, lui cria: - Tire la chevillette, la bobinette cherra.	La bonne Mère-grand qui était dans sont lit à cause qu'elle se trouvait un peu mal, lui cria: - Tire la chevillette, la bobinette cherra.

Grojuif tira la chevillette et la porte s'ouvrit.	Le Loup tira la chevillette, et la porte s'ouvrit.
Il se jeta sur la pauvre femme et la dévora en un instant, car pour satisfaire ses instincts sanguinaires, Grojuif tuait et dévorait par plaisir.	Il se jeta sur la bonne femme, et la dévora en moins de rien; car il y avait plus de trois jours qu'il n'avait pas mangé.
Ensuite, il ferma la porte et s'étant revêtu des vêtements de Vérité,	Ensuite il ferma la porte,
il se coucha dans son lit et	et s'alla coucher dans le lit de la Mère-grand,
attendit l'arrivée de Doulce France.	en attendant le petit chaperon rouge, qui quelque temps après vint heurter à la porte.
- Toc! toc!	Toc, toc.
Grojuif contrefit à nouveau sa voix.	
- Qui est là?	- Qui est là?
Doulce France, bien que surprise par le ton	Le petit chaperon rouge, qui entendit la grosse voix du Loup, eut peur d'abord,
de la voix mais sachant sa	mais croyant que sa Mère- grand
grand'mère enrhumée, répondit: - C'est votre petite Doulce France.	était enrhumée, répondit: - C'est votre fille le petit chaperon rouge,
Elle vous apporte des galettes et un petit pot de beurre.	qui vous apporte une galette et un petit pot de beurre que ma Mère vous envoie.
Adoucissant sa voix,	Le Loup lui cria en adoucis-

Grojuif lui cria: - Tire la chevillette, la bobinette cherra.	sant un peu sa voix: - Tire la chevillette, la bobinette cherra.
Doulce France entra.	Le petit chaperon rouge tira la chevillette, et la porte s'ouvrit.
Grojuif la voyant lui dit en se cachant dans son lit:	Le Loup, la voyant entrer, lui dit en se cachant dans le lit sous la couverture:
- Pose les galettes et le petit pot de beurre sur la huche et viens près de mon lit.	- Mets la galette et le petit pot de beurre sur la huche, et viens te coucher avec moi.
Doulce France fut étonnée de l'allure étrange de sa grand'mère.	Le petit chaperon rouge se déshabille, et va se mettre dans le lit, où elle fut bien étonnée de voir comment sa Mère-grand était faite en son déshabillé.
- Ma mère'grand, comme vous avez de grands bras!	Elle lui dit: - Ma mère-grand, que vous avez de grands bras!
Grojuif reprit sa voix naturelle et répondit:	
- C'est bour mieux t'emprasser, ma ville...	- C'est pour mieux t'embrasser, ma fille.
- Ma mère'grand, que vous avez de grandes jambes!	- Ma mère-grand, que vous avez de grandes jambes!
- C'est bour mieux gourir, mon envant.	- C'est pour mieux courir, mon enfant.
- Ma mère'grand, que vous avez de grandes oreilles!	- Ma mère-grand, que vous avez de grandes oreilles!

- C'est bour mieux t'égouter, mon envant.	- C'est pour mieux écouter, mon enfant.
- Ma mère'grand, que vous avez un grand nez! - C'est bour mieux renifler les bedides affaires ma ville.	
- Ma mère'grand, que vous avez de gros yeux!	- Ma mère-grand, que vous avez de grands yeux!
- C'est bour mieux te foir mon envant.	- C'est pour mieux voir, mon enfant.
- Ma mère'grand, que vous avez de grandes dents!	- Ma mère-grand, que vous avez de grandes dents!
- C'est bour mieux te groquer...	- C'est pour te manger.
Et sur ces mots Grojuif s'élance sur Doulce France pour la dévorer.	- Et en disant ces mots, ce méchant Loup se jeta sur le petit chaperon rouge, et la mangea.
Mais elle recula épouvantée d'avoir eu confiance en un tel monstre: elle appela à l'aide.	
Un des fils de la nouvelle France courut à son aide et arriva juste à temps pour délivrer Doulce France des doigts crochus de Grojuif.	
Et dans l'azur, la "Vérité" de ses chauds rayons, put emplir le ciel de France pour se mêler à la clarté de la nouvelle Europe.	

Appendix Three

L'HOMME AUX MAINS ROUGES (Anon.)

Il y avait une fois un homme qui était le maître d'un immense pays très peuplé, possédant de grandes richesses naturelles.

Mais par malheur pour lui, cet homme avait les mains couleur rouge sang, cela le rendait si laid et si terrible qu'il n'était ni femme, ni fille qui ne s'enfuit devant lui: on l'appelait: l'HOMME AUX MAINS ROUGES...

Il était fourbe, menteur et cruel, et son peuple en souffrait beaucoup.

Ayant remarqué une jeune femme parfaitement belle, appelée EUROPA, il la demanda en mariage; cette union le tentait surtout, car en l'épousant il devenait le maître de la moitié du monde.

La Princesse EUROPA n'en voulait point, car elle avait peur de ses mains rouges et, d'autre part, on savait qu'il avait épousé jadis d'autres femmes et qu'on ignorait ce que ces femmes étaient devenues par la suite.

Toutefois, grâce à une politique habile, l'HOMME AUX MAINS ROUGES était arrivé à séduire plusieurs Dames de la Cour de la Princesse EUROPA et, influencé par celles-ci, qui s'appelaient FRANCIA, ESPANA et d'autres encore et aidé dans son entreprise par un ancien prétendant à la main de la Princesse et, évincé par celui-ci, et connu sous le nom de JOHN BULL, il parvint à capter la confiance d'EUROPA et celle-ci accepta d'écouter ses propositions.

Il la reçut avec toutes les marques de déférences dues à son rang et lui fit visiter tous ses domaines.

Il possédait une très grande étendue de terres et de nombreuses villes, dont quelques-unes de toute beauté, ainsi que d'immenses champs de blé et des mines de métaux divers d'une grande richesse.

Finalement il la conduisit dans son magnifique château du KREMLIN et lui confia les clefs de tous ses domaines en lui disant: "Si vous écoutez mes propositions, vous serez la maîtresse de toutes mes terres et de tout mon peuple, mais il y a une seule condition: c'est que vous ne pénètrerez jamais dans mon château de Katyn et que vous n'entrerez jamais dans la chambre secrète, dont voici la clef, car s'il vous arrivait d'en ouvrir la porte, il n'y a rien que vous ne deviez craindre de ma colère."

La Princesse EUROPA promit de lui obéir et il partit seul pour visiter ses grands domaines de Sibéria.

La curiosité est un vilain défaut et malgré toutes ses qualités, la Princesse EUROPA était une petite curieuse et d'ailleurs elle ne comprenait pas que l'HOMME AUX MAINS ROUGES eut des secrets pour elle, puisqu'il voulait l'épouser.

Comme vous l'avez probablement deviné, dès qu'il se fut éloigné, la Princesse EUROPA fut si pressée d'aller voir ce qu'il y avait dans le château de KATYN qu'elle s'y fit conduire immédiatement et qu'elle faillit se rompre le cou en courant dans les escaliers; aussitôt arrivée devant la chambre secrète, elle prit la petite clef et ouvrit la porte en tremblant...

Tout d'abord, elle ne vit rien car tout était obscur, mais tout à coup, elle s'aperçut que le plancher était couvert de sang et que les corps de plusieurs femmes étaient pendus le long des murs!

C'était toutes les femmes que l'HOMME AUX MAINS ROUGES avait épousées et qu'il avait égorgé (sic), l'une après l'autre, car elles n'avaient pu résister à la curiosité de voir ce que leur époux leur cachait si soigneusement; il y avait là, la malheureuse Princesse POLONIA, la jolie Grande Duchesse LITHUANIA, etc.

La Princess EUROPA pensa mourir de peur et sa petite main trembla tellement qu'elle laissa choir la clef sur le plancher... Hélas, elle tomba dans une mare de sang et se tacha.

Affolée, la Princess EUROPA s'enfuit et se renferma dans sa chambre où elle essaya de nettoyer le sang qui était sur la clef, mais elle eut beau frotter, le sang ne s'effaçait pas plus que sur les mains de l'HOMME AUX MAINS ROUGES.

Lorsque celui-ci rentra de voyage, il redemanda les clefs de ses châteaux et autres domaines... hélas, il s'aperçut bien vite que la clef de la chambre secrète du Château de KATYN, manquait au trousseau!

Il entra dans une violente colère et s'écria:

> 'Par l'âme damnée de LENINE, mon maître, tu vas te préparer à mourir, EUROPA! car tu as découvert mon secret et ton peuple sera sous ma botte! J'en ferai des esclaves!'

La Pauvre Princesse EUROPA s'enfuit à travers les innombrables couloirs du château et monta sur la plus haute tour d'où elle appela son Peuple à son secours, mais personne n'osait affronter la colère du terrible HOMME AUX MAINS ROUGES.

Tandis qu'elle scrutait l'horizon, anxieusement, elle entendait crier au bas de l'escalier:

> 'Voulez-vous bien descendre, ou je vais monter là-haut!'

'Encore un petit instant, Monseigneur, disait-elle...' et elle interrogeait toujours l'horizon, car elle avait vu un nuage de poussière avancer sur la route; hélas, ce n'était qu'un troupeau de moutons...

La voix de l'HOMME AUX MAINS ROUGES se faisait plus proche, la Princesse EUROPA se crut perdue! Mais soudain, son coeur se mit à battre d'espoir! Là! sur la route, galoppant à une vitesse fantastique, elle vit arriver une troupe de cavaliers! C'était le noble Prince GERMAIN qui, suivi de quelques valeureux fidèles, choisis parmis les meilleurs combattants de son peuple et des peuples voisins, accouraient au secours de la Princess EUROPA!

Ce fut un beau spectacle! Au moment où le cruel HOMME AUX MAINS ROUGES allait égorger la belle EUROPA, les portes du château volèrent en éclats et le Prince GERMAIN entra, l'épée haute en criant:

'Défends-toi, si tu l'oses! Ignoble STALINE!' (car c'était là le nom de l'HOMME AUX MAINS ROUGES) et après un dur combat, au cours duquel le Prince Germain et ses fidèles, montrèrent des prodiges de valeur en luttant contre les partisans de l'HOMME AUX MAINS ROUGES, ils purent enfin écraser celui-ci et rendre la liberté au Peuple opprimé et à la belle Princesse.

Peu de temps après, la princesse EUROPA se mit sous la protection du vaillant Prince GERMAIN, son sauveur, pour son bonheur et celui de son Peuple.

De longues années de Paix et de Prospérité furent alors assurées au Monde entier.

En voilà terminée, l'histoire merveilleuse et véridique de l'HOMME AUX MAINS ROUGES!

Appendix Four

THE COLONIES IN VICHY PROPAGANDA FOR CHILDREN

Et si vous preniez un avion géant, qui vous emmènerait au-delà des mers et des océans pendant des jours et des jours, pendant des semaines et des semaines et pendant votre vie toute entière, vous n'auriez pas fini non plus de voir et d'admirer toutes mes forêts, toutes mes rizeraies, tous mes cacaoyers, tous mes palmiers, tous mes bananiers, tous mes arbres à caoutchouc, tous mes palais blancs et toutes ces terres immenses, cinquante fois, cent fois, mille fois, plus étendues que celles que vous pouvez contempler ici et qui se trouvent encore là-bas, sous un ciel qui est mon ciel, ces terres infinies où des centaines de milliers de bouches murmurent mon nom à chaque seconde: la France, la France, la France!...

And if you were to get on a huge aeroplane that would take you beyond the seas and the oceans for days and days, for weeks and weeks, and for the whole of your life, neither would you have time to see and to admire all of my forests, all of my paddy fields, all of my cocoa plantations, all of my palms, all of my banana trees, all of my rubber trees, all of my white palaces and all of these immense territories, fifty times, a hundred times, a thousand times bigger that those you can see here, and which are also, over there, under a sky that is my sky, these never-ending lands where hundreds of thousands of mouths murmur my name every second of the day: France, France, France!...

(Nohain, J., op. cit., p. 22).

The political and strategic importance of the French colonies during the Second World War, recognised by all sides involved in the conflict, meant that some prominence was given to the overseas territories and their peoples in the propaganda campaigns of Vichy France. The *Service d'information* of the *Secrétariat d'Etat aux Colonies* was very active in informing the French people about their more far-flung relations, not only through the essentially superficial medium of posters, but also through travelling exhibitions, such as the '*train-exposition des colonies*' which toured the country in 1943. The slogan of this exhibiton '*L'Empire uni derrière le Maréchal*' [The Empire united behind the Maréchal] encapsulates the major function of most references to the Empire during this period; that of consolidating the image of national unity and latent strength that was at the root of so many propaganda offensives at this time. After the attack on the French fleet at Mers-el-Kébir in the summer of 1940, and the British/Free French operation to take Dakar and the West African colonies (Operation Menace) in September of the same year, the colonies also provided a setting in which to portray the treacherous and violent nature of the enemies of the state.

Despite having a relatively high profile in propaganda for adults, however, no detailed study has yet been made of the role the colonies play in children's literature during this period. The extract quoted above is the only direct reference to the colonies to appear in the short stories analysed in detail, but comics of the period, particularly the very aptly titled *Siroco* (Clermont-Ferrand, 12 December 1943 - 27 July 1944) would appear to represent a more fruitful terrain for such research . In non-fiction, a text like Piquet's *L'Empire Français et les pionniers*,[1] appears to be

1 Piquet, V., *L'Empire Français et les pionniers*, illustrations by Henri Dimpre, la Publicité Synchronisée, Paris, Editions CPRN, Imprimerie Alfa, Lyon, n.d.

representative of the educational/picture book approach most often favoured, a similar combination of didacticism and entertainment being adopted in board games such as the *Le Voyage impérial*, created by Alain Saint-Ogan for the '*Service des manifestations*' in 1941.[2] The only other occasion on which the colonies feature in the propaganda literature for children discussed in this study, is in the accounts of Pétain's life referred to in Section IV. Here, some space is devoted to Pétain's pacification of the 1925 revolt in Abd-el-Krim (Morocco) and the Rif War that ensued. Despite the fact that his intervention led to this part of Morocco passing from Spanish to French control, however, the imperial aspect of the conflict is of only secondary importance in all of these accounts. For Pétain's hagiographers, the principal motive in retelling these events is the greater glorification of the Maréchal's military and diplomatic talents, and an emphasis on his repeated willingness to respond to the Nation's regular appeals for his assistance.

2 See Gervereau, L., 'Y a-t-il un 'Style Vichy'?' in Gervereau, L., and Peschanski, D., (eds), *La Propagande sous Vichy 1940-44*, Collection Publications de la BDIC, 1990, p. 143.

Bibliography

PROPAGANDA TEXTS CONSULTED

BDIC: Bibliothèque de Documentation Internationale Contemporaine, Nanterre
BN : Bibliothèque Nationale, Paris
CDJC: Centre de Documentation Juive Contemporaine, Paris
VEF : Bibliothèque Municipale, Vichy, fonds Etat Français

Anon, *Abécédaire*, Bureau de Documentation du Chef d'Etat, Imprimerie Draeger, 1943 [V EF 371.5 43 B].

Anon, *Abécédaire à l'usage des petits enfants qui apprennent à lire et des grandes personnes qui ne comprennent pas encore le français...*, G. Mazeyrie, Paris, n.d. [CDJC B 5297].

Anon [N], *Il était une fois (L'Histoire de Doulce France et Grojuif)*, Illustrations by JB, NEF, [1942] [BDIC France 15/16 littérature enfantine O pièce 22908].

Anon, *Jeanne D'Arc. Sa mission, son exemple*, Edition du Secrétariat Général de l'Information, n.d. [V EF 371.3 s.d.].

Anon, *L'Homme aux mains rouges*, n.d., (Censorship n°5, P.A. 033 994 AFPA 6171) [BDIC S pièce 11345].

Anon, ['un instituteur'], *L'Instituteur et son rôle dans la restauration de la famille française*, Secrétariat d'Etat à la Famille et à la Santé, Commissariat Général à la Famille, Paris, L'Office de Publicité Générale, Société industrielle d'imprimerie, n.d. [V EF 372 s.d. F].

Anon, *La France que nous aimons. Documents destinés à la décoration des salles de classe, octobre à décembre 1942*, Information de l'Etat Français, 1942 [V EF 371.3 42 F].

Anon, *Le jeu du drapeau*, Vichy, Wallon Ed CPRN, [1943] [BDIC France 2 N 263/20/1-3].

Anon, *Maréchal Pétain, Chef de L'Etat français*, Office Central de l'Imagerie, 1941, Accord de la censure no OA 237 [V 1941].

Anon, *Présentez armes! Les Voyages du maréchal*, Cosmos, n.d., Autorisation Vichy OA 245 [V EF 371.3 s.d.].

Anon, *Vercingétorix, la belle histoire de la France*, Illustrations by Pierre Luc, Paris, Editions Artistiques et Littéraires, Imprimerie E. Desfossés, 1943 [V EF 371.3 42 C] [BN 4° L^{39} 1183 (1-3)].

Anon, *Youpino*, NEF, n.d. [CDJC 5498].

Bauer, E., *Trau keinem Fuchs auf grüner Heid, Und keinem Jud bei seinem Eid!* Stürmer-Verlag, Nuremberg, 1936 [CDJC 7892].

Benjamin, R., *Le Maréchal et son peuple*, Plon, 1941 [BN microfiche 8° LN^{27} 81990].

Bertrand, J., [Henry Babize] and C. Wacogne, *La Fausse éducation nationale. L'Emprise judéo-maçonnique sur l'école française*, Centre d'Action et de Documentation Anti-maçonnique, n.d. [CDJC 761].

Chéronnet, L., *Les Artisans de la ville et du village*, Paris, Office central de l'imagerie, 1943 [BN 4° R pièce 3965].

Coston, H., *Les Corrupteurs de la jeunesse. La main-mise Judéo-maçonnique sur la presse enfantine*, Bulletin d'information anti-maçonnique, Centre d'Action et de Documentation Anti-maçonnique, n.d. [BDIC France 15/16 littérature enfantine S pièce 11360].

Crassé-Sceillier, *Un jour de fête*, Editions 'Alsatia', Paris, 1942 [BN 8° Y^e pièce 111333].

Dancette, V., *Il était une fois un pays heureux*, Illustrations by P. Baudier, Les Editions de la Générale Publicité, 'Pour le Bureau de Documentation du Chef de l'Etat', [1943] [V EF 371.3 43 D].

Dancette, V. and Jacques Zimmermann, *La Bête est morte. La guerre mondiale chez les animaux*, illustrations by Calvo, Editions de la Générale Publicité, 1945, Autorisation no 472 Co. no. 11.02.82, 2 vols [Private collection].

Descouens, R., *La Vie du Maréchal Pétain racontée aux enfants de France*, illustrations by Mario Simon et Francis Dujardin, Editions de la Vraie France, Imprimerie de 'l'Eclaireur de Nice', [1940], Visé par le Service Central de la Censure No. 10,379 [V EF 371.3 n.d.] [BDIC France 15/16 enseignement F pièce 2567].

Estienne, Y., *La Belle histoire d'un chêne*, Cover by A. Desroches, illustrations by M. de Montfalcon, Editions de la Revue 'Les Alpes', 1 rue Villars, Grenoble, [1942], Censure texte 2516 OA 364, gravures QO 24530 à 24555 [V EF 371.3 1942] [BDIC France 15/16 littérature enfantine Q pièce 4311].

Hansi, L'Oncle, [J.J. Waltz] *L'Alsace heureuse, la grande pitié du pays d'Alsace et son grand bonheur racontés aux petits enfants par l'oncle Hansi avec quelques images tristes et beaucoup d'images gaies*, Floury, 1919.

Hérault, P., *La Vie d'honneur du Maréchal Pétain racontée et illustrée pour les jeunes français* (text and illustrations), Farré et Freulon, [1940] [BDIC France 15/16 littérature enfantine Q pièce 4166].

Jaboune [Jean Nohain], *Bonjour la France!*, poems by Christian Schwaebel, illustrations by Emmanuel Cocard, Collection de Tobby l'Eléphant, Société d'Edition, façonnage et impression, Villeurbanne, Presses Giraud-Rivoire, Lyon n.d., No. de censure OA 333 [V EF 371.3 s.d.].

Paluel-Marmont, A., *Il était une fois un Maréchal de France*, illustrations by Pierre Rousseau [and Germaine Bouret], 'Edité par Fanfan la tulipe, journal pour enfants', les Editions et Publications Françaises, Imprimerie Curial- Archereau, [1941 and reprinted 1943?]. [V EF 371.3 s.d.] [BDIC France 15/16 enseignement gr f. pièce 360].

Paluel-Marmont, A., *Pétain*, Librairie des Champs-Elysées, Imprimerie Blanchong, 1942 [V EF B Pet 42].

Paluel-Marmont, A., *Six petits enfants et treize étoiles*, illustrations by Lucien Boucher, Editions et Publications Françaises, Paris, 1942 [BN 4° Y^2 pièce 741].

Pellos, *Vive le sport*, illustrations by Pellos, Commissariat Général à l'Education Générale et aux Sports, Vichy, 1942 [BN 8° V pièce 27157].

Pétain, P., *La France nouvelle. Principes de la communauté. Suivis des appels et messages 17 Juin 1940 - 17 juin 1941*, Paris, Fasquelle, 1941.

Pétain, P., *Le Maréchal vous parle*, Lyon, Blanc & Demilly, 1940 [BDIC France 2 O pièce 22708].

Piquet, V., *L'Empire Français et les pionniers*, illustrations by Henri Dimpre, la Publicité Synchronisée, Paris, Editions CPRN, Imprimerie Alfa, Lyon, n.d., Autorisation no. 142 [V EF 3713 s.d.].

Reynaud, J., *De Vercingétorix à Pétain. Le Don de soi-même*, Illustrations by Jean Chièze, Editions de la Générale Publicité, Paris, Pour le Bureau de Documentation du Chef de l'Etat, Imprimerie de Croutzet et Depost, 1942 [V EF 371.3 42 C].

Vincent, P., *La Belle aventure du Disque Rouge*, Illustrations by Gad, Imprimerie Curial-Archereau, Paris, 1945, [BDIC France 15/16 littérature enfantine Q 4704].

Select Bibliography

Agathon, *Guidargus du livre politique sous l'Occupation (1940-1944)*, Paris, 1990.

Amouroux, H., *La Grande histoire des Français sous l'Occupation*, vol 2, *Quarante millions de pétainistes*. Laffont, 1977.

Bettelheim, B., *The Uses of Enchantment. The Meaning and Importance of Fairy Tales*, Penguin, 1976.

Bruno, G., [Augustine Fouillé], *Le Tour de la France par deux enfants. Cours moyen*, Belin, 1877 (1978 facsimile of the first edition).

Cazals, R., (ed), *Les Ecoliers de Tournissan 1939-1945*, Privat, 1978.
Chalas Y., *Vichy et l'imaginaire totalitaire*, Actes Sud, 1985.
Citron, S., *Le Mythe national: L'Histoire de France en question*, Flammarion, 1987.

Delarue, P., 'Les Contes merveilleux de Perrault et la tradition populaire' in *Bulletin Folklorique de l'Ile de France*, Oct-Dec 1951.
Delarue, P., *Le Conte populaire français*, Paris, 1957, 2 vols.
Deronzier, R., *Il était une fois... le livre d'enfant!*, Edition Point-image, Paris, 1986. [the most notable feature of this book is that it neither investigates fairy tales nor does it mention the Second World War!].

Ellul, J., *Propaganda. The Formation of Men's Attitudes*, Vintage Books, 1973.
Emmelina, J., 'La "littérature" de l'école primaire. L'idéologie des livres de lecture courante dans l'enseignement primaire, en France, depuis la IIIe République', in *Idéologie et propagande en France*, Picard, 1987, pp. 171-190.

Faure. C., *Le Projet culturel de Vichy*, Presses universitaires de Lyon, 1989.
Fouché, P., *L'Edition française sous l'Occupation*, Paris 7, 1987, 2 vols.
Foulkes, A.P., *Literature and Propaganda*, Methuen, 1983.
Fromm, E., *The Forgotten Language. An Introduction to the Understanding of Dreams, Fairy Tales and Myths*, Holt, Rinehart and Winston, 1970.

Gervereau, L., and Peschanski, D., (eds), *La Propagande sous Vichy 1940-44*, Collection Publications de la BDIC, 1990.
Giolitto, P., *Histoire de la jeunesse sous Vichy*, Perrin, 1991.
Girardet, R., *Mythes et mythologies politiques*, Seuil, 1986.

Halls, W.D., *The Youth of Vichy France*, Clarendon Press, 1981.
Hazard, P., 'Comment lisent les enfants' in *Revue des deux mondes* no. 42, 1927, pp 860-882.

Kramnick, I., 'Children's Literature and Bourgeois Ideology: Observations on Culture and Industrial Capitalism in the Later Eighteenth Century', in Perez Zagorin (ed), *Culture and Politics from Puritanism to the Enlightenment*, Berkeley, 1980, pp. 203-240.

Leriche, M., 'Les Contes dans l'éducation des enfants de 6 à 11 ans, ou l'Heure du Conte', in *La Revue du livre et des bibliothèques*, no. 12, 1934, pp. 261-272.
Lüthi, M., *Once Upon a Time. On the Nature of Fairy Tales*, Indiana University Press, 1976.

Miller, G., *Les Pousse-au-jouir du Maréchal Pétain*, Seuil, 1975.

Ory, P., *Le Petit Nazi illustré. Le Téméraire (1943-1944)*, Editions Albatros, 1979.
Ozouf, J. and M., 'Le Thème du Patriotisme dans les manuels primaires' in *Mouvement social*, Paris, no. 49, 1964, pp. 5-31.
Ozouf, R., *Le Nouveau statut de l'école et du personnel enseignant primaire. Recueil de documents officiels*, Editions FN, [1941].

Perrault, C., *Les Contes de Perrault*, illustrations by Pierre Noury, Flammarion [?1923].
Perrault, C., (ed G. Rouger), *Contes de Perrault*, Garnier, 1967.
Perrault, C., (ed M. Soriano), *Contes*, Garnier-Flammarion, 1991.
Propp, V., *Morphology of the Folktale*, Indiana University, 1968.

Ragache, G., and J.-R., *La Vie quotidienne des écrivains et des artistes 1940-1944*, Hachette, 1988.
Renonciat, A., *Petit Poucet dans la jonchée des feuilles*, Le Vieux Papier, 1990.
Renonciat, A., *Livre mon ami: lectures enfantines 1914-54*. (Catalogue établi et rédigé par Annie Renonciat), Mairie de Paris, 1991.
Rioux, J.-P. (ed), *La Vie culturelle sous Vichy*, Complexe, 1990.
Rossignol, D., *Histoire de la propagande en France de 1940 à 1944*, PUF, 1991.

Soriano, M., *Les Contes de Perrault, culture savante et traditions populaires*, Gallimard, 1977.
Stephens, J., *Language and Ideology in Children's Fiction*, Longman, 1992.

Thalmann, R., *La Mise au pas. Idéologie et stratégie sécuritaire dans la France occupée*, Fayard, 1991.

Van Gennep, A., 'De la valeur pédagogique des contes de fées' in *Revue Bleue*, Paris, 1921, no. 19, pp. 602-606.

Zipes, J., *The Trials and Tribulations of Little Red Riding Hood*, Heinemann, 1983.